DOLLY MIXTURES

*These pieces have been shortened to fit on the CD. The complete versions are contained in the accompanying book. Recorded in Dolly's Cottage by Andrew Wilson. Sound editing: Andrew Wilson, Órfhlaith Ní Chonaill and Shay Leon. Disk reproduction: Shay's Studio, Loughrea, Co. Galway.

Dolly Mixtures

(Voices from Dolly's Cottage)

An Anthology of Prose and Poetry from

Writers' Ink
Creative Writing Workshop

Edited by Órfhlaith Ní Chonaill M. Phil.
(Creative Writing)

Available from:
www.writersinksligo.com

First published in 2005 by Writers' Ink,
Strandhill, Co. Sligo, Ireland.
e-mail: orfs@iol.ie
Writers' Ink is an affiliated workshop of
Amherst Writers & Artists:
www.amherstwriters.com

Cover design by Andrew Wilson

Printed by Paceprint Ltd., Dublin 4
www.paceprint.ie

ISBN: 0-9550443-0-8

ACKNOWLEDGEMENTS

I offer my sincere thanks to the following people:

To Pat Schneider for developing such an excellent model for creative writing workshops and for giving me the courage to start my own.

To Mary Molloy for the idea of using Dolly's Cottage as a place to write.

To the members of Strandhill Irish Countrywomen's Association for the use of Dolly's Cottage and for their kindness to us over the years.

To all of the writers who have participated in Writers' Ink Workshops, for the fun, the companionship and the wonderful writing they have done and shared.

To all of the writers who submitted work for *Dolly Mixtures*; the standard of submissions was impressive.

To Nuala Niland for typing poems and manuscripts.

To Maeve McCormack for sourcing printers and organising the ISBN.

To Andrew Wilson for the cover design, for the recording of the CDs and for his help with editing prose pieces to fit on disk.

To Mel Howes for her expertise with computers and for her calm in times of crisis.

To Peigín Doyle for the proof-reading.

To Hugh MacConville for financial advice.

To Shay Leon for editing the CDs.

To Padraic and Geraldine Killoran of Kelly's Pub, Strandhill, for hosting a book launch.

Finally, to the late Dolly Higgins for the spirit of simplicity and geniality that is her legacy and is part of the atmosphere of Dolly's Cottage.

Genius is hidden everywhere; it is in every person, waiting to be evoked, enabled, supported, celebrated. It is in you.

Pat Schneider

Writing Alone and With Others

Contents

FOREWORD

Órfhlaith Ní Chonaill

This book is a celebration of a great writing experience that has been happening in Dolly's Cottage, Strandhill, over the last four years. As facilitator of Writers' Ink creative writing workshops, it has been my privilege to work with a very talented group of writers. They come from all walks of life and from all corners of the globe (as you'll hear by the accents) and they travel from as far away as Cavan and Donegal to attend the weekly workshops.

When we duck our heads to enter the low door of Dolly's Cottage, we step back in time and we enter sacred space. The fire is crackling in the hearth, the plates are gleaming on the dresser, ancient fossils are embedded in the flagstone floor. There is no ceiling above us, only the thatch and a little St. Brigid's cross that nestles there, crafted by the original roof-maker, to protect the cottage from fire. St. Brigid is there, in her magic cloak, St Patrick is banishing snakes. Here, we put away our everyday lives and become, simply, writers. It is in this atmosphere that many of these poems and stories were evoked and shared. Our first responses were gentle, saying what we liked or admired in the writing and what moved us. Later, several of these pieces were brought back for rigorous critiquing sessions where consensus was never found, but the writers got an insight into how their work could be interpreted (or misinterpreted) by others.

It was the excellence of the work being produced that created the demand for this book and made it possible. The standard and volume of submissions for the anthology reinforced my belief that this writing deserves and needs to be shared with a wider audience. This book has been written by thirty-six people. Some of them have never been published before. In the spirit of equality that exists within the group, I have decided not to include biographies. I believe that the voices from Dolly's Cottage will speak eloquently for themselves.

On an editorial note, I need to say that the writers were the final arbiters in what was and wasn't changed in their pieces. Where writers were unready or unwilling to accept my suggestions, I resisted the urge to edit as ruthlessly as I would edit my own work.

LOST SHIPS FROM THE ARMADA

T.N. Treanor

The noise in the car was oppressive. As soon as they were on board the ferry she put on her coat and climbed to the left-hand deck. She knew that the weather would probably keep him in the car and, anyhow, he was listening to some old cackle on the radio.

The boat wasn't long in leaving. She supposed there was never too much traffic at this time of year. Had the rain eased? The wind continued to blow strongly from the direction of the ocean. The Shannon was green. Not the superficial chlorophyll green of the wet fields visible over in County Clare, but sterner, angrier, accusing. As the ferry rounded the head of Tarbert Island the wind struck with more force from the west. Each raindrop was like a tiny thumbtack pressed into her face and quickly removed before blood was drawn. She contemplated returning to the car. Pulling her coat up to her neck, she decided to endure the crossing on deck, watching the churn of the water. There was a tanker, with lights, far out on the estuary. The power stations on the Kerry and Clare sides were smoke-belching sentinels, at odds with the rural scene. Pylons graced the skyline, conducting their precious cargo to Ballylongford and beyond.

The small ferry was buffeted as it crossed the river. Seven cars, one with a horsebox, and one delivery truck. Probably a good number for the season. She tried to calculate how much this crossing had earned for the ferry company, and how much they would pick up in the day. The mathematics was too complicated and she gave up.

He joined her on the narrow deck. His sports jacket was insufficient for the weather. He should have buttoned it, at least, and turned the collar in, but she knew he wouldn't. It flapped around in the wind, causing him a further discomfort.

"You can hardly see toward Limerick, what with the rain."

He was looking upriver. She turned round, looking east also.

"Where does Kerry finish and Limerick start?" she asked.

"Not sure."

She turned to face the river again. The greenness remained secretive. She hoped to see dolphins, but couldn't discern anything. Their brief chat provided a lyric to the sound-track of the wind and the boat's engine.

"Imagine who might have sailed these waters over the years. Pirates maybe, from Africa or Scandinavia."

"British frigates."

"Missionary monks."

"Grace O'Malley."

"Lost ships from the Armada."

They left the familiar conversational game as quickly as they had joined it. She could tell he was getting uncomfortably wet.

"I'm hoping to get to Galway before dark," he said, as if he should just mention it.

She didn't move and kept looking out at the sea.

"Don't wait to the very end," he said, before returning to the noisy car. She waited as long as she could. The ferry neared the northern quay, and she went down the greasy steps to the car deck.

The ferry boat struggled to the quay, forced westward by the strength of the river. The river which had flowed under the bridge at Dowra, gently crossed Lough Ree between Lanesborough and Athlone, calmly observed the new houses being built on the Clare and Tipperary shores, and been forced through sluice gates at Ardnacrusha before reaching the drowned river valley. At this time, and on this day, the ocean provided only minimal resistance. The power of the moon and the sun provoked tidal opposition at other times. The heat of the sun had warmed the sea in the Caribbean and directed the currents north-eastwards. Despite the wind and rain, there was a temperance in the estuary that afternoon, not usual for the latitude.

The ferry docked safely for the fifteenth time that day, discharging its load, while eleven cars waited patiently to cross southwards from Killimer.

LANDSCAPE

Sacred landscape

Hear the blur of wings

Recall the sky darkened with flying shapes

Remember the wonder of their multitudes

As you stand looking skywards in your garden

Your sacred landscape of childhood

At that magic hour of twilight

At the end of a summer's day

When the sun's heat still glows on your face

And the summer air fills your hair with sweetness

Paula Gilvarry

GRANNY GLITTER

Carol Jane Wilson

My granny had a motto in life: "Sew another sequin on your frock, Mary Anne!" It used to puzzle me at the time, because my name isn't Mary Anne, it's Caroline. I eventually found out that there was an old music-hall song that had a line in it, "Throw another chair-leg on the fire, Mary Anne," but my Granny had fearlessly adapted it for her own use.

She loved anything that sparkled or glittered. Granny was drawn to glitter like a magpie: she hung prisms in the window to make rainbows and dancing lights on the wall, and pinned big diamanté brooches on her everyday frocks.

She always wore bright colours. "We're long enough dead, dear!" she would say if anyone twitted her about it. "No need to go into mourning before we have to!" she would add with gusto.

Granny had a button box full of wonderful buttons and would get them out on rainy days so I could look at them. If she didn't like the buttons on something she got new, she would cut them off, and replace them with something gaudier, or more exotic, from her button box. "There, that's more like it!" she would say with satisfaction, holding it up so I could see the new buttons when she had finished sewing them on.

If her everyday clothes and jewellery were exuberant, they were as nothing to her get-ups for when she was going out, down to the workingmen's club on a Saturday night. She would dazzle you with acres of sequins, clanking costume jewellery, great big pearls, or fake gold chains. Granny used to haunt the charity shops and the market stalls. She would buy remnants and make them up herself. People gave her bits and pieces, or else she would buy things from the catalogue, paying them off at so much a week.

The sparkle of her personality out-glittered anything she had on her back or round her neck. She was an irresistible force. No one could help enjoying themselves around her; she radiated vitality and a compulsion to happiness. She should have had, stuck on her forehead, whatever the opposite of a government health warning is – a 'get well here!' sign, or something. If you could have bottled her, you would have got it made.

Sometimes, she drank port and lemon, other times a glass of stout. High days and holidays, or if someone was paying who could afford it, she had her favourite, a brandy and Babycham.

"Come on, girls, get those knees up!" she'd yell, as soon as the music started to play anything halfway lively. She'd be in there, arms like hams round anyone near to her, getting the party going.

Granny was the soul of generosity and compassion. If she thought you needed it, she would give you the shirt off her back, sequins and all, and you couldn't argue, or even try to thank her. Many's the night she sat up with someone sick or dying, or held the hand of a woman through her labour.

No one who came to the door ever went away without a cup of tea inside them and a bit of whatever food she had in the house. She had so little herself, but what she did have she spread around so liberally that it was like the miracle of the loaves and the fishes every day.

I was always welcome in her house. It was there I took my troubles and my joys when my mother was mad at me, or just too busy to have time for me. Dad had died when I was small, so my mother had a hard enough time bringing me up alone.

For everything from skinned knees to broken hearts, gold stars to finding ladybirds, Granny was always there, big and comforting. No trouble or joy was too small or too big for her attention. She made good things better by the way she entered into and shared them so fully. She drew the poison out of bad times by the same method. I always came away soothed, comforted and restored in myself.

She started to ail almost imperceptibly, fading so slowly that, for quite a long time, people could fool themselves that it wasn't happening.

She lost weight, masses of it. I didn't realise the significance of it. Half the adult women I knew were talking wistfully about reducing, so I vaguely supposed it was what she wanted. No one disillusioned me.

It was coming up towards Christmas. The school was looking for dressing-up clothes and such, to make costumes for the Nativity play. Granny gave them most of her sequinned frocks. It didn't feel right. It felt like ice melting in my stomach. "But what are you going to wear when you go out, Granny?" I asked her, anxiously.

"Sure, I couldn't wear them anyway, you'd get two of me into them," she said with her old cheerful grin. "Don't you worry about me, I won't be needing them any more!" I must have looked unconvinced, because she added gently, "Can't I get some more, better than ever, when I've finished slimming?"

That year, our school had the best-dressed Nativity play for miles around. The three kings were especially sumptuous in Granny's adapted cast-offs. No one enjoyed it more than Granny did.

That was her last Christmas. Early in the New Year, she died. Not a word of complaint had passed her lips, so it came as an appalling shock to me. The very foundations of security in my life had vanished, leaving me in a cold, dark place. I couldn't stop thinking about Granny and crying in corners, privately to myself.

I kept thinking about the funeral. I was used to funerals; in those days children were. There was no nonsense about it not being appropriate for them to go. You just went along and got on with it. It was the bit about ashes to ashes, dust to dust that upset me about Granny. She'd been so colourful and sparkling in life, how could she be connected with anything as grey and colourless as dust or ashes? It bothered me.

Then I had the idea. It wasn't long after Christmas, so I knew where everything had been put away. I went to look and there it was, right where I thought it would be. I knew we had some left over. I took it out carefully, put it in my coat pocket and felt a bit better for the first time since Granny died.

The funeral was the next day. The flowers were lovely, masses of them. Everyone came. Everyone loved my Granny. She had been such a beacon of cheerfulness; it was like a light had gone out over the whole neighbourhood. Many others besides me would miss her.

I went through the service in a fog of numbness, one hand holding my mother's, the other in my coat pocket, clutching tight. I was past crying. I felt unreal.

We filed out to the graveyard and followed the coffin to the open grave. We were at the front with at least a hundred and fifty people crowded in behind us. Finally, we got to the bit about dust and ashes. My mother let go of my hand and bent over to get a handful of earth. I didn't bend over. Instead, I took my hand out of my pocket and carefully prised the lid off the little tube. I stepped forward and scattered my silver glitter down onto the coffin.

"What are you doing?" my mother gasped and started forward in horror. The vicar held up his hand to stop her. "She's paying her own very special tribute to a very special lady!" he said with infinite kindness in his voice and, crouching down to my level and looking into my eyes, he added, "Your granny would have loved it, wouldn't she?" I couldn't speak, I just nodded, but I loved him for his understanding of me and of my Granny.

That night, there was a big do at the workingmen's club, a sort of wake for Granny. It was what she had wanted. She had even left a bit of money behind the bar to start it off, paying in a bit week by week, when she could spare it. "I want it to be the biggest and best knees-up ever. Give me a right good send-off!" she'd said, and so it was. People talked about it for years, and dated other events from their relation to it, as in, 'that was in the spring after Granny Glitter's wake' and so on.

When they were clearing out Granny's house, my mother gave me the button box. She said Granny had wanted me to have it. For a time, I couldn't bear to open it, or even look at it. I hid it under my bed and forgot about it.

One day, I was looking for something that had rolled under the bed and I came across it. I was scared at first and I looked at it sideways for a while. Then I reached out a hand and slowly opened it. The contents sparkled and winked at me. They brought Granny alive again in a rush of feelings. I could hear her saying gleefully: "Sew another sequin on your frock, Mary Anne!" and I could see her doing it. As I tipped out the gay assortment of buttons and ran my fingers through them, lifting them up and letting them fall in glittering showers, I felt soothed and warmed and comforted. I was able to think about Granny again, and be glad that I had known her, as well as sorry I had lost her.

I have her box of buttons to this day. On rainy days, or days when I feel rainy inside, I get them out and look at them, and remember my Granny, and feel better for thinking of her. And when I buy new clothes, I look at the buttons and, if I don't like them, I cut them off and sew some others on out of the button box. Then I say to myself: "There, that's more like it!"

EMPTY SPACE

I can see him now, not old, not yet,
rising slowly from the chair in the shade of the tree,
the chair he so skilfully crafted from wood, decades ago.
I see him shuffle along the short stone paved path
through the back door, taking for ever, it seems,
to reach the back room where I wait impatiently,
with my thoughts, wondering why I am here.

He drops in his easy chair, reserved without notice
and begins to hum a tune I know
from days long lost to his wasted mind.
Who does he see sitting here across from him
in the back room, his domain for a decade now?
I could be anybody come in for a chat
or perhaps I am somebody from the past,
hidden away in a chamber for ever forgotten.

Suddenly the tune stops and his eyes search mine
for some trace of something familiar or lost,
and I ask, 'You alright there?'
pleading for some sign of recognition.
'Yes' he says,
returning to the tune with a hint of a smile
and he nearly knows who I am.

Paddy Donoghue

THE BOOBY PRIZE

Maeve McCormack

Boobs, boobs, boobs. Breasts, bo-zooms. Mammary glands. Bras, corsets, vests. Pert, saucer-like, wibbly-wobbly wonders. Fascination. Beauty and allurement. Nurturing and feeding. Comfort. Sex and pornography. Exploitation. Ladies' breasts. Breast is best. All women get them at some point. Some men too. Some women lose them.

Do all cultures have the same fascination with breasts as we do? Feed them, cosset them, pack them, nurture them? They mean different things to different people. Young girls wait for them to arrive. Boys too. Most of them can draw them, (probably in secret) well before they develop them. If they come too soon, the girl gets self-conscious; but if they come too late, she gets self-conscious too. When they do come, she has to get a bra – who does this with her? Does she do it on her own? Developing breasts are a sign of physical maturity, like menstruation, part of the rite of passage from girlhood to womanhood.

Attitudes to breasts are changing all the time. In the past, depending on Edwardian, Victorian, Jacobean or Elizabethan fashions, you showed them off or you didn't. Perhaps the same attitude is found inside the head of every woman. We all remember getting hair under our armpits, our first period and our first bra. Probably a matter of pride at the time, but how did we behave in the school changing rooms? Did we change under a tee-shirt or bare it all? Were we being modest or self-conscious, or learning to be ashamed of our bodies as the big cover-up began? Girls wear bras. Nice girls don't show cleavage. Breasts should be seen but apparently not SEEN.

Girls grow up. They discover strappy tops, pretty bras, bikinis. They can do this all on their own; they don't need boys or men or mothers or fathers or teachers to point out that they have breasts. Nor do they need these people to tell them what they should feel about their breasts.

A body is a body. We all have different parts. My breasts have seen the sun in Spain, they have swum in the Rio Negro in Brazil. They have been stroked, licked and cosseted by more than one man. They have fed children. They have flopped into bed after a hard day's work. They have been bathed, dusted and dressed; made me feel sexy and good and loved. They have been carefully examined by doctors and - the real booby prize - removed.

I don't have them any more. I mourn their passing. I miss them. But I am alive. I look at other people with breasts, and other people looking at other people with breasts. Why does society try to monopolise them; decide how you should wear them, what shape they should be? The bad side of humankind will always seek something to exploit. I know in my heart and soul, breasts are part of women and, no matter how much society tries to mistreat or mislead us, we will always treasure that part of our womanhood.

But I have a more urgent worry. I am pregnant – how will I feed my child?

SOFA

Save it, she thought.

Save what?

Her sad personal tale.

She looked out the window

into the light haze,

the garden after rain.

If I cannot save myself,

how can I save him?

She watched him fidgeting

under the weight of his own expectations.

Climbing into the large deep sofa,

she snuggled down, wanting warmth.

Drifting in and out of snoozes,

thoughts, thrashing here and there,

jogged memories

that had been lost for years.

Tall trees, dazzling,

leaves falling and floating.

His movements slow, even weak.

In carefree days, her heart

with the power of a lion,

clawed for him.

She had mastered this great talent,

to see it slip, slowly, painfully,
almost urgently, away.

Lying still, she let out a weary gasp,
seeing him, the great man,
plunging feet first against the flow.
Save what? she cried aloud.
Silently, she lay again enjoying the comfort
of her large, deep sofa.
She thought of tall trees, dazzling,
holding her tight
and making her feel high.

Outside her window
night had fallen,
and all above were
the bleeding stars.

Mary C.H.

THE MOON WEAVER & THE BEETLE

Peigín Doyle

Dohbarkhan, god of malice, blew a spattering of raindrops down upon a chrysanthemum pod and drew back to watch the blossoms shiver in his breath. His face was white as a mask and blue as an indigo shell. His breath was a curling frond of mist that ribboned across the lacquer-black sky.

Deep in the shelter of a bamboo tree, a shy green beetle rolled home a ball of passion-flower gum to her nest. Baby beetles looked solemnly through their beetle-black eyes at Dohbarkhan's smiling spite and knew it was a good day to be a beetle, too absurd for a god to play with.

Plum, pomegranate, persimmon and pearl shimmered on Katiki's headdress. She shuffled delicately across the courtyard, bewitching to the eye. Baby beetles sighed for her. Too good, too good to escape the god, they agreed, while they watched the slow progress of their food as it was rolled across the glistening leaf.

"Har-ra, har-ra," they cheeped, so low that a breeze blew their whispers away.

Dohbarkhan heard the wind rustle and spotted the thought it carried. He swam out across the sky and floated lazily on the air currents, his yellow eyes gleaming.

In the courtyard, Katiki, the Moon Weaver, worked at her loom. She wove stars for the night, gold threads for the dawn, and wondered when the pattern would spin itself out. She shivered and prayed to her mother.

Beetle mother cocooned her children and drew down a sheltering leaf. Gods' playtime was no time to be about. Her thin forelegs clicked a prayer to the great earth.

"Har-ra, har-ra, Life-giver. Don't leave her weaving her own misfortune. Snap the thread and let her spin a different life to the one she is bound to weave."

A sudden gust of wind blew through the clearing. It whirled around Katiki's head, buffeting her. A door to her sleeping room slammed shut.

The beetle looked up from her nest and saw that, around them, the bamboo grove was still. She looked across the space to where Katiki sat at her loom. In the humid stillness she felt the tremor of rushing power. Calmly, she clambered from her hidden nest, laying a silken thread across the leaf to guide her back to her babies if they called. Spreading her transparent wings she flew to the Moon Weaver and planted a stinging kiss on Katiki's cheek.

There was blood now on the cloth Katiki was weaving. She was hurt by the insect's sting. No creature had harmed her like this before – only people, and she had withdrawn from them a long time ago. Before this, abandonment and loneliness were the only injuries she had suffered and they had never drawn blood. She wondered why the beetle had stung her.

Katiki sensed a presence, a power, hovering near her loom. Then it was gone. Masking her bloodied cheek, she left the loom and walked quickly to the sheltering verandah of the temple.

On the far side of the mountain, an old man drew his last breath but held it and turned back from the vast peace that had been drawing him in. He took another tiny breath and lay, suspended between life and death, in his daughter's hut. A woman groaned as the baby in her womb lodged in the breech and stopped being born. Shadows closed over the forest and leaf-gold raindrops pattered down.

The world lived and died by Katiki's weaving. When her thoughts wandered, life and death were suspended, awaiting the prompt of her shuttle. She was the mute guardian of living things.

In the afternoon haze the bamboo trees shifted lazily. The baby beetles fell asleep in their camouflaged nest. The mother beetle flew to Katiki's shoulder and nestled beneath a blossom on her embroidered robe. She wondered if Dohbarkhan could see them.

Blue shadow and white light danced fleetingly where normally she saw only the comforting darkness of wooden beams. At the end of the verandah, in the shade of the latticed walls, the fire in the hearth guttered beneath its bronze cauldron.

The beetle flew to the hearth and bit into the fibre rope that held the suspended water pot. A twist, a ravel, a sudden buck of the handle, and water cascaded onto the glowing hearth stones.

Billowing steam raced past Katiki, like it knew where it was going. It chased along the verandah, searing Dohbarkhan's exploring fingertips. Katiki followed the wisps of vapour as they curled around the turn of the verandah. On the north side of the temple, everything was cold.

The beetle's action had thrown her between Katiki and Dohbarkhan, like a particle of light caught between bludgeoning passions. She lived in a world of huge vegetation, gigantic forests, leaves that stretched like vast plains, breezes that blew around her like storms. The delicate girl was a giant in her eyes. But her calm compassion drew her to protect Katiki, and Dohbarkhan followed like a sailor to a beacon. A wise god would have loved and respected this beetle, but Dohbarkhan had more cunning than wisdom and dismissed anything less than his surging power.

In the clearing, nothing stirred. The west wind blew by, a stranger to the land, drawn from its usual course by the sudden stillness it sensed in the East. It came to sniff the air, peer over the trees and mountain tops, and learn what had blotted out the rich smells and sounds that blew from those latitudes.

A great laziness hung abroad. Down, so far down the wind had to swoop low to see it, there was a hint of movement. Strange currents snaked around a solitary temple courtyard. It plucked the shutters and sent the dormant air scudding crazily. There was a black-blue tint to the air. It exuded energy – not goodwill. It was seeking something, like a child seeks the underbelly of a tiny insect – out of crushing, heedless curiosity.

The wind peered to see what was in the shadows. It was curious now, alert and probing. A girl was there, shrinking back, yet unafraid, with soft glad eyes. And there was a sound. Thrrr. Thrrr.

The west wind heard the slam of a door, the hiss of steam and that thrrr-thrrr of insect wings. The dark blue current recoiled, enlarged and re-folded itself in billows, grew dense and black, then spread itself like a dancer's fan and lifted itself up over the tree tops. The wind sent a fresh moist gust to rattle the courtyard. It rose and swirled around the mountain. All around it was stillness.

The dying man pulled greedily on its cooling breeze. The wind moistened his parched mouth. Trees quivered, relieved to feel movement in their deep trunk cores. But, when the wind passed by, that stillness crept back and lassitude blanketed the village. Out of the surrounding forest crept a small tendril of vine. It hooked itself into a crack in the stone paving and held on to its small conquest.

Katiki stood on the verandah, pondering. Always her strength had glowed like a dim lamp behind a screen. "The beetle stung me and I left the loom. I could feel great power close to me. But where is my place in this?" she asked herself.

"I am not afraid of anything in this world," Katiki told herself. "The loom holds me close. That was the pact I made. I would release my mother from her loom. I would spin and weave everyone's story. I am not a slave, yet I am bound to stay.

"My world is small but I make it rich with my colours. I stitch flowers, nuts, berries, leaves and blossoms. Sometimes, at night when the world is sleeping or just before the storms come, I leave my loom and dream my story in my own wild way. Then I see gazelles walk with panthers and cranes play with flying fish. I laugh aloud at them and they enjoy me too.

"But my mother roams the world and the skies now. Riding the back of night clouds, she sometimes brings me stories; images of faces; funny endearing anecdotes of humankind.

"People are the only creatures I don't approach. They are good but undisciplined. They don't realise how they hang suspended in my threads. I care for them. I tend to them. I don't know why. Perhaps it's because I saw my mother dying in her servitude to the loom. My mother had released her mother before her, and she before that, right back, mother to daughter, to the first one who had stepped down from the rain-spattered sky one night and walked with a young human.

"He was vigorous but innocent. He knew nothing of wisdom or of the mystery beyond his hunt for food and shelter. Moon mother could have despised his ignorance and left him in disgust. But she looked at him and saw – a child. It was a simple child, who laughed and smiled and cried and never grew up and never knew how needy it was or how quickly it would die without nurture. And my ancient moon mother pitied him, and the other people, in their rough shelters.

"She took her loom then and set it in the forest clearing, measured out the threads and looped them to the starry frame. The warp threads were life, growing, learning, children, sustenance, old age, death.

"Across the frame she threaded wefts of silver, gold, starlight and rich colours. Awareness was dark or bright but always gleaming. Insight was a pale pinky gold like sunrise. Knowledge was deep, strong shades. Spirit was like silver on the afternoon sea. Wisdom a deep, deep gold. Humility an opalescent blue. Sympathy was a warm reflection of her own colour. Acceptance a melting green. Mindfulness glowed rich amethyst.

"Even in their barbarism, love was always the humans' colour. It's what she sensed in them, what drew her to them that starry night," she thought.

So the ancient Moon Weaver set up her loom. She threaded the fibres. She held the shuttle and sent it from side to side. But, unlike her other tapestries, she didn't lay down the pattern for long. Knowingly or unknowingly, people picked and wove their own colours into the Moon Weaver's gauze.

In the beginning there was light and dark. The darkness was everywhere, lifted only by flashes of love.

The cloth played out slowly through the loom. Bedrock. Continents. Mountains. Forests. Oceans. Over millions of lives, new colours appeared. The shades lightened. Subtle hues lit the darker outlines and gave richness and contrast. Flowers, fruits and villages appeared in the engagement of warp and weft. Still the Moon Weaver sat and tended the unfolding pattern of life.

One day, her daughter called her home and she left the loom. Then bright colours ran over the cloth. White. Ice blue. Sea green. The world and the people froze in diamond brightness. The Moon Weaver felt pity but would not return.

Her daughter stepped down and took her place and wove the world back to life and laughing children. The icy beauty retreated.

So it went on: millions and millions of lives; daughter following daughter. Those daughters became more earth than moondust. Their silver glow turned to creamy peach. Their dark hair gleamed of nuts and red earth, rather than black lacquer sky. The warp and weft, the unrolling bolt of cloth, reached into their being and wove the weaver into their own tapestry. Moon Weaver and earth became one. She became alien to the stars and sky, except for that huge well of insight that still inspired the love and pity of her task.

Dohbarkhan was a volcano's whelp. Reared in bubbling melt and torrid menace, he was spat out in sulphur and stench. The plumes of the volcano were like the rage of a god. The smoky grey-black clouds held a merciless heart.

In this furnace, Dohbarkhan grew malignant and mischievous. He felt whole only when the seething power terrified the world, and birds' hearts failed. Then Dohbarkhan swelled in the sense of its unbridled omnipotence. His world was a black storm where he basked in dust and doom.

Dohbarkhan was only interested in the lower world when something caught his attention. The beetles' thought had drawn him to Katiki and he had stayed, fascinated by her brightness. But now, the beetle mother's defiance had enraged him.

He burst out from the light-tipped forest and snatched one of the baby beetles. He spread its wings to gaze into their silver sheen and touch it with his curved golden nail.

The baby beetles rasped in terror. They rubbed their legs and agitated their wings like blossoms in a high wind.

"No. Don't. Hurt. Help. Sister. Mother! Mother! Mother!"

The west wind swooshed back over the nest, agile and alert. It whipped the whispering pleadings of the babies onto its hurtling back and carried them high.

On Katiki's shoulder the mother beetle flew up from her embroidered sanctuary. Wild and startled, she made towards her nest. An unseen force pushed her back. She strained against the invisible barrier, beating her wings.

Dohbarkhan played with her. He curved his fingertip inward in a beckoning movement and the air receded. The mother beetle flew forward. With outfaced palm, Dohbarkhan pushed outward and she was repulsed. She heard her babies' cries but could not reach them.

Her wings beat in increasing desperation. It seemed she might fall and die from the effort and never reach home.

Katiki roused herself from her long musings. Down all the aeons of her loving bondage she had watched the ways of gods and humans and kept apart. She knew their faults. She had guided the shuttle. She did not demand obedience. Together she and the humans wove their destiny.

In all that time the gods had stared and played their tricks on people and never noticed that the tiny beings they made sport of had loved, cared, understood and forgiven. They had taken meaning and insight into their lives.

Now the gods seemed strange, brute creatures to Katiki. Her own moon mother ignored their heavenly cacophony and turned her cool compassion on the earth instead. Their power wasted, the gods were reduced to beautiful creatures who blazed and turned in gorgeous futility.

Between the two worlds, Katiki was marooned. She loved her mother and was bound to the loom. She cared for the world's creatures but could never be one. Yet she would never sport with them like the playful gods.

Now her earth and heaven had collided.

Katiki did not think beyond the agony she felt in her heart. It echoed the thrrr of the beetle's frantic wings. Dormant energy pushed her fingers. Snatching her shuttle, she threw swirling pink of western sunsets over the warp and weft. Arcs and billows of pristine colour swooped over leaf-green threads. The west wind thrashed the forest fronds and shook the passion-flower tree.

Dohbarkhan held his ground. Shards of vermilion flame split the black sky. Lightning broke around Dohbarkhan's hand. He ignored it. He impaled the baby beetle on his golden fingernail and stroked its diaphanous wings. He shivered in delight as he felt her terror.

With a desperate sweep of her hand, Katiki spilled the cones and spools of coloured thread into the story. Dark storms spread along the pattern. Black, red, orange, sulphur and grey.

Katiki worked frantically. She heard the frightened babies and it maddened her. Past, future and her own destiny were all forgotten. Even her moon mother meant nothing to her now.

People would die, she knew. But it had to be. To claim its god, the volcano must be allowed flower over the life patterns.

The cloth bucked and twisted in turmoil, straining the cords that secured it to the loom. Black covered green. Blue light chased through the rippling fabric. A smell of sulphur filled the forest.

A roar burst from over the horizon. Burning clouds came to envelop the volcano's god-child. Ribbons of viscous red twined around him. Ash blindfolded him and cinder dust swaddled him.

A last hank of thread lay on the ground. Katiki snatched it up. Bright airy blue spilled across the confused mêlée. It poured down through the layer of sulphur to reach the deep green forest. It swooshed beneath and around dots of emerald. Lifting a heddle, Katiki tore them from the cloth.

In that instant the rising west wind blew dust into Dohbarkhan's eyes and snatched the beetles from him. Up they rose, the green beetles borne by rushing jets of blue, over the trees and beyond the clearing. The mother's wings beat even faster than the wind. She thrust forward on bruised webs, reached her babies and covered them, protected them.

Katiki did not send the shuttle from side to side but watched it take its own course. The story it told was a dazzling, shifting kaleidoscope. The bamboo leaves whipped and danced. Black clouds and red lightning flashed and were carried down the fabric and off the loom.

Far out to sea, the volcano bellowed and cradled Dohbarkhan deep in its molten depths. He sank into the stench and revelled again in its unstoppable power. Spreading his gold nails luxuriantly over the orange torrent, he melded with its savage energy and was home. He thought no more of the humble beetle or the intriguing iridescence of her wings.

Now green, blue and white streaks tumbled through the tapestry. In union with the rushing wind they raced down the cloth and up into the high sky. The fabric strained within the warp and weft and tore off the frame in a cascading ferment.

Katiki dropped the shuttle. Her fingers ached and she shook from her struggle. She looked around the clearing. Tattered bamboo leaves were scattered over the courtyard. Warm and soothing, the east wind returned and flowed over the startled greenery. Away in the distance, a new-born baby cried.

Stretching her shivering arms, Katiki reached up and removed her headdress. She looked at the ornate stitches for a moment, then placed it on the ground beside the shattered loom. She spread her fingers and pushed them through her loosened hair.

The west wind flew on, carrying the beetles away from the eastern gods. When they were far away, it gently set them down with a friendly eddy and blew onwards. In time the baby beetles grew older and spread further, until they could be found in every part of the earth. They are still calm and persistent.

Katiki turned her back and walked away from the clearing, to make her own story. She walked without counting the steps. Sometimes, her mother walked with her and they told each other stories. At the shores of a great lake, she watched the flying cranes and laughed for joy.

COWBOYS AND INDIANS

Celluloid screen met fantasy
where sylvan bank met stream
deep in Cappard wood.

Mounted on foot, weaving,
dodging, avoiding enemy arrows,
confident that courage never fails;

Sure that right, as strong,
overcomes wrong, as weak.

Never flinching, never doubting
that Grand Canyon, buffalo
and Texas ranch spread on
south Slieve Aughty slope.

As ivy, a parasite on trees,
reality preys on dreams.
Cappard wood is no more.

Dermot Lahiff

ASH

Mel Howes

A familiar voice said: "Ash tree, only good for burning."

Bernie looked around but there was no one near. She was standing on the small, rocky summit above the top field, taking in the early morning view. Her breath formed clouds that tripped and bundled their way down the slope to join their denser parents along the stream below. The sun was just peeping over the horizon a few miles distant.

Bernie's mind wandered from shopping lists to DIY lists, on to gardening lists and back to shopping again. She knew, somewhere in her mind, there was something important happening today but, somehow, the incessant list-making was taking priority.

Slowly, she picked her way down the hill and across the field, careful not to turn her ankle in the hoof-marked ruts. The dew-strewn spider webs glistened like a million tiny diamonds studded across the rushes.

"Autumn's here," she said aloud, inwardly chastising herself for talking aloud while alone. It was bad enough, all this getting older, without senility or madness creeping in as well.

Back at the house she put on the kettle for tea and opened a can of food for Rex, her regal Siamese, who wound himself around her ankles as if hoping to trip the food down to him more quickly than it would otherwise appear.

"Well, it's nice to feel loved," she said aloud again. "Damn!" – now she couldn't tell if that was out loud or just in her head. She took a deep breath and made the tea, placing the two cups, milk, sugar bowl (all the way from Torquay, a present from a neighbour a few years ago) and teapot onto the tray.

Treading lightly, she ascended the stairs, being careful not to spill anything. Outside the landing window she admired the tall ash, its leaves dancing in the breeze as they fell to the ground.

She quietly opened the bedroom door and stepped in. At the sight of the empty bed, the flowers and the black suit hanging on the wardrobe door, she sobbed and dropped the tray. She remembered what she had to do today.

MISTRESS IN A BOTTLE

You and your mistress,
Do you remember when it began?

Were you on a date
that day in your youth,
the day you shattered the glass door
that locked you out?

Was she in your car
that night in your twenties,
when you and the dog were jailed,
not fit to be driving?

When you brought her along
handshakes turned to fist fights,

trusts were betrayed
friends abandoned
    jobs terminated
        homes pillaged
            lovers battered
                families rejected.

She
provided solace,

warmth,

like a mother's unconditional love.

Now

    the dog is dead

    you are old and

    she leaves you cold.

You

    are

        living

           for

               nothing.

Don't ask for pity.

Don't ask for forgiveness.

Don't ask for sympathy or understanding.

I

    feel

        for

           you

               nothing

Nothing–

except Love.

Pauline Howard

JOE MCDONALD HAD A FARM

Kevin McGloin

The pitiful Friesan calf stood shivering under a whitethorn bush where it had sought shelter from the freezing east wind. Joe McDonald watched it for a while; its legs seemed to have grown longer as the body shrank due to severe malnutrition. He went over and gave the animal a few taps with a hazel stick. The calf moved forward with stiff, unsteady steps, the entire frame rigid as it moved. After a few steps the calf stopped and, lowering its head to the ground, coughed painfully. Joe made a mental note to get word to the guys who collected dead and worn-out animals. If he was lucky he might get a few pounds as the calf was young and might be passed off by some unscrupulous butcher.

A sudden burst of morning sun brought the temperature above freezing for the first time that morning. Icicles that hung from the corrugated iron roof of the byre glistened and began to drip water. Joe went around to the yard and opened the barn door. A flock of Rhode-Island-Red hens surged out into the morning air, like prisoners being let out for exercise. The sight and sound of the chickens as they careered around the yard gave him a fleeting sense of joy. They seemed enthusiastic for life, vibrant and noisy, in contrast to the atmosphere of gloom that had descended on his own life. The chickens cackled and fluttered around the yard for a while then drifted back to the warmth of the barn to begin another shift.

Joe took a basket and gathered the morning's crop of eggs, then got a bag of meal from the pantry. The chickens fought for a share as he distributed the food. After putting some water into trays that were scattered around the floor, he switched on the lights and bolted the door.

When things began to go wrong with the dairying business, a neighbour across the Border in Fermanagh had introduced Joe to the 'battery-hen' concept. The Rhode-Island-Reds were put on a twelve-hour shift and production went up by one hundred per cent. Twice a week, the eggs used to be smuggled across the Border, where the price was higher and there was a ready market. At the end of the month he used to collect a cheque which, together with the few pounds of dole money, used to keep him solvent for another while.

Getting a bucket from the pantry he went to milk the one remaining cow, the last of the dairy herd. The cow had given two gallons after calving; today there was barely two pints. He poured the milk into a can, putting the last cupful into a bowl for a scrawny cat that purred around his legs looking for its share. He aimed a few half-hearted kicks at the cat which dodged the heavy boot and dived on the bowl of fresh milk. After milking the cow, he went over to a lean-to and pulled some hay from a bale and tossed it into the cow's stall. The offspring had already been sacrificed so that its mother would give milk for another couple of weeks.

It had taken eleven years to get from the point where he had milked sixty cows and worked fourteen hours a day. A half-finished, slatted shed rotted in testimony to his earlier ambitions.

Joe himself would have been happy to plod along on the small farm his father had signed over to him but the advisers descended on him with bundles of plans. Expand or go under was the gospel of the time. Increase your acreage, increase your quota, borrow and build. He was a young man then. He bought the neighbouring hundred acres with a sizable bank loan and arranged a generous overdraft. Guys with striped suits arrived at the farm on a daily basis. Taking a pair of wellies from the boot of the car they used to walk the land with him, preaching their gospel as they went. Samples were taken and sent off to Dublin for analysis: more nitrogen on that field; more potash on the other. The field at the back needs lime; the one beside it needs drainage. Trucks arrived with tons of fertiliser and lime. Machines drained the fields as quickly as a man could walk. He built up a herd of pedigree Friesans and the milk cheques soon rolled in. The bills and repayments followed.

Joe worked long hours and, although the cash was flowing out faster than it was coming in, he felt a certain sense of satisfaction with his achievements.

The first sign of trouble came when he received an invitation from his bank to come in and review progress.

"There's a plateau in your overdraft," the lady at the bank told him. She shuffled his statements on a polished mahogany desk, explaining the bank's theory on how an overdraft should operate. "Peaks and troughs, Mr McDonald." She scribbled a rough graph on a sheet of paper. The result looked like a bad lightning storm. He rubbed his hands together and stared at the polished desk, awaiting her advice. She gathered the papers and put them in a buff folder. "You can have a think about our discussion," she told him, getting up and extending her hand.

A week after this meeting the first cheque bounced. He quickly sold off some of the cows and paid the proceeds into his account. Some time later there was another invitation.

"I think it might be best if we converted your overdraft into a loan account," the lady told him.

Joe had no choice but to agree with her strategy. "Whatever you think is best," he told her. There were several more meetings, and more of the herd was disposed of, culminating in him signing documents to facilitate the bank in selling off the land he had bought. He knew that his dairying enterprise was falling apart but there was nothing he could do to reverse the decline. Soon the bank wanted to dispose of the entire farm and house to settle the remainder of his debt. Joe ignored all further communications, but attended some more meetings with the lady who was handling his account. He kept one cow for milk and sold off the remainder. With some of the cash he prepared the barn and bought one hundred ready-to-lay chickens.

Two days after Christmas, Joe's father died in the local nursing home. One of his brothers was already home from England, staying with his wife's relatives down the country. The other brother, who had married an Indian girl in Birmingham, was contacted and came home the next day. After the funeral the three brothers sat around a table in a local pub and reminisced on times past. The three had gone out with three sisters one glorious summer when Joe was in his late teens. One by one, the three sisters and his two brothers went off to England.

"You should have come over," they told him.

"I suppose I should have," Joe said and rubbed his hands together.

Twenty-three years had gone by since that memorable summer. She had written to Joe a couple of times asking him to come over.

"My father's not well," he told her. "In a few months when he improves, I'll join you." The first time she came home Joe hardly recognised her. She had dyed her brown hair blonde and drank vodka like it was spring water.

When he got the final notice to vacate the house and farm, at a specified time on a specified date, Joe felt like a man who had been on death row for years and at last the hour had come. It was the end of the line, nothing more could be done. He had lived with the nightmare for so long that he felt a sense of relief to have the whole situation taken out of his hands at last.

When the hour of reckoning was close at hand he took his single-barrelled shotgun from its place on top of the dresser, and put a few cartridges in his pocket. A framed black and white photograph of the family had stood on the mantelpiece for as long as he could remember. He took the photograph in his hand and stared at it for a while, then threw it in the fireplace before leaving the house for the last time.

He made his way to a vantage point on a hill overlooking the house and he sat himself down behind an old stone wall. He had visions of the sheriff charging up the lane on a white horse, followed by his deputies, like they did in the old westerns. When the sheriff did come, he was led by a white Ford Mondeo with a blue light on top, followed by a furniture van, a saloon car and another white Ford Mondeo with a blue light on top. He placed the barrel of the shotgun on the wall and watched his house being ransacked. The sheriff's party carried off everything of any value and put it in the furniture van, then boarded up the windows and put a hefty chain with a padlock on the door. Several boxes were brought to the barn. The chickens put up a stiff resistance. They did not go quietly into the night, but squawked and cackled in vain. A heavy chain and padlock was put on the gate before the cavalcade left.

Joe made his way back to the house and just stood there, looking at what was once his father's and mother's pride and joy. A deep sense of failure and remorse overcame him.

The lights of a car shone through the dusk as it turned off the main road and headed towards him. He quickly put a cartridge in the gun and held it to his shoulder. The old cat was about forty yards away, sitting on the stump of a sycamore tree. When he squeezed the trigger the cat flew into the air as if it had suddenly sprouted wings, then landed on the ground like some object that had fallen from the sky. The tail twitched a couple of times before it died.

Taking the gun by the barrel he swung it angrily. The butt smashed against a stone pillar and splinters of polished beech flew into the air. He then swung the gun around over his head and let go. It landed on the roof of the house with a clatter, and slid down, coming to rest on the flat roof of the kitchen.

When the car pulled up beside him, Joe eased himself into the passenger's seat. The driver leaned over and kissed him briskly.

"I hope we don't run into traffic in Dublin," she said, without taking her eyes off the road. "We haven't much time to spare."

Joe took a sideways glance at her, always prim and business-like. In all their meetings at the bank he had never once seen her smile. On the main road she brought the car up to sixty. Joe leaned back in the seat and tried to imagine their flight to Boston. He had never been on an aeroplane before.

IMAGINE

Imagine, I said out loud to myself,
I thought I would die
when she walked out the door,

I mean really die
not just the ordinary die,
the 'I wish I was dead' die
or 'I feel like I'm dead' die.
No, I'm talking about the real die,
the face down in the lake die
with the note in the bumbag
strapped to your waist die,
and the weight of the nothing
in your heart die.
The corpse and the funeral type of die.

Imagine, I said out loud to myself,
I thought I would die
when she walked out the door.
But I didn't.
Instead, I slipped sideways
into someone else's dream.

Mitzie O'Reilly

THE SATURDAY NIGHT CALF

Maura Gilligan

The red heifer had surrendered to her labour pains and finally sat down, pushing out the calf's black feet. There was no rush. The night was calm and mild, and the Plough and his other starry relations shone behind the silhouette of the dark hill before us. The heifer had chosen the hollow at the bottom of the field, and the other cattle clustered around her in the darkness, aware of her anxiety. Her breath fell heavily on the still, misty air.

We waited by the old elder tree and talked quietly now and again. We said: "Come on girl, good girl," and shone the torch on her progress every few minutes, rejoicing at the sight of the little black nose that appeared next. Willie gently tied the rope around each foot and, with a firm downward pull, helped to ease the little calf's entry into the world. She slid out, all shiny and new in the light of the torch. Willie cleared a bubble of mucous from her mouth and her mother began to lick her into wakefulness, stimulating her tiny, thin body. Such a little thing she was, and what long legs she had, and a beautiful face with a white star, just like her mother's, on her forehead.

The other cattle moved off slowly into the darkness, as if they knew the excitement was over for now. We stayed an hour with them, cow and calf, while the stream flowed with soft sounds behind us, and an occasional night bird flew by. We left them to go for a pint, and the stars shone above the black hill.

Returning two hours later, we found the little calf still warm, but dead, flatter somehow as if her mother had accidentally sat upon her. Our sadness echoed the darkness that the mist had thrown down.

Willie buried the stiff black and white body of the baby calf in the earth's dark brown cradle. So perfect, she lived only three hours. The red cow roamed in sorrow for days, returning again and again to the place where the calf had been born.

RELEASE

A sea-otter lies on Port Salon sand
in swimming pose. Clare turns him over–
his body not yet stiff, sleek from head to tail,
face to one side, whiskers bristling.

She touches him as she would an old friend
on his wake bed, spreading webbed claws
between her fingers – comfort in familiarity
of fur, form and sinew.

Our shadows curl over him,
helpless as the ashes of a last letter
let go on the wind, surfing off with a seagull
out of vision, carrying our questions:

what allowed him drift into death,
journey at ebb tide to this place of rest,
allowed him float with animal ease,
while an aunt clings to life
in her ninety-eighth year, body eager
to escape, her will unable to leave?

Anne T. O'Connell

GRASS

Andrew Wilson

It was a wonder of nature, right there outside their cottage window. Every day the growing disparity between the uncut meadow grass and the lawn-mown neatness in front of it only amazed them more. Not just the height (some of the grasses now reached two-and-a-half foot) but the variety of species. Even from indoors you could pick out at least five different colours and forms of gently waving grass-flower fronds.

In all the years they had lived in the cottage, they had never before left the meadow uncut and ungrazed by horse or cow. But this year they had purchased a lawnmower and had carved a patch out of the sward, where they could sunbathe or picnic. This had introduced a touch of suburban order into the landscape, which now lay tamed and low before the wild clumps beyond.

Until now, they had always given in to their neighbour's suggestion that he put his livestock into the field, "to keep it down for youse". At first it had been a novelty to see a full-grown horse up close, to make tentative contact across the temporary electric fence, to wonder as it raced and bucked around this new bit of space and food, or rolled around, legs flailing. A morning of watching cows revealed a very different, ruminant pace, a complex programme of movements, feeding, lying down and socialising.

Afterwards, the horse's offerings would be carefully gathered to feed the rhubarb but the cow-pats were more problematic; runny, soggy patches that were impossible to remove fully before the grandchildren came looking for their very own football pitch. Cowpats, they agreed, were not what they used to be; the crusty piles remembered from childhood excursions into what had been, for them, the foreign land of the countryside. If the book on organic gardening was to be believed, today's cow-pats were so full of antibiotics that you would hesitate to put them anywhere near your vegetable patch or compost heap.

This year however, they had avoided seeing Séamus for the annual 'negotiation'. When eventually cornered in the post office, they told him they wanted to let the grass grow "at least until July," to let it set seed, and only mow it in time for the meadow to green up, before the grandchildren and the football.

"You're welcome to the hay when we do cut it or, if you'd rather, we could get it baled for silage."

"Ah no, you're all right, we'll leave it so."

But they could tell Séamus was not pleased. His need was for more grass now. The one field he had left was stretched to the limit with the animals he had on it. A couple of dry weeks with no growth would leave his animals hungry.

"We want to create a wildflower meadow," they offered by way of explanation.

"To manage it the way it used to be," he said.

"Wouldn't it be lovely if a corncrake came back to nest there. One was seen in Easkey last year!" she added.

"Sure, if a corncrake came back, a cat'd have him for sure!" Séamus said as he walked off, leaving them to reflect uncomfortably on their own cat's prowess at hunting, not to mention the feral cats that plagued the local wildlife.

They knew they could expect to see Séamus walking his land and looking over the fence with disdain for their blow-in ambitions and foolish wastefulness. Still, they would not be deflected. They were not obliged to feed their neighbour's cattle, after all. But it was another post in the invisible fence of cultural difference that only gradually revealed itself to the in-comers who were lulled by the illusion of a shared language.

It was a month later and the fecundity of grasses had even overpowered the buttercups. They had cut a path through from the mown section at the front of the cottage to Séamus' field so they could assuage their guilt over the cows' hunger, by tipping the grass mowings over the fence. The greediness with which these offerings were received was a double rebuke to their sensibilities.

The whole herd used to race down Séamus' field the moment they heard the lawnmower start up and wait impatiently for the first load of cuttings. It was hard to give them all an equal share. There was a definite hierarchy. Try as they might to throw the clippings further out to the younger or weaker beasts, the bullies always shouldered the weak aside or even kicked backwards at any attempt by them to reach the sweet stuff. Was this normal bovine behaviour or evidence that they were all too hungry? It took an effort of will and much discussion to stick to their guns and preserve the meadow's bounty.

From the path through the grass, they could see the great variety of wildflowers that were sending spindly stalks up through this west of Ireland jungle canopy to flash their colours through the green. There were buttercup, burdock, vetch, and knapweed, as well as tiny flowers they couldn't quite identify from books.

A small girl, who was visiting with her mother, wandered up the path and almost disappeared in the wilderness. The cat could bound no longer through the grass to its accustomed toilet patch, nor was there the distressing sight of patches of feathers or bunny fur in his favourite killing places. They wondered if, perhaps, a hare might be taking shelter unseen in the richness, especially now the surrounding fields were being cut for silage. On fine evenings they listened for the cry of a returning corncrake. They agreed that it might take a year or two for the birds to discover the new haven, even if it were big enough to tempt them.

By late June the meadow was starting to look untidy. Summer storms had laid parts of it down. The tops of the grass were blond and ripe and clumpy, with rusty spires of dock seeds here and there. In July they asked a neighbour to bring his ancient Ferguson tractor with a sidebar cutter. It took only half an hour to lay the sward low, in bold stripes of wilting grass and flower that browned to hay in the hot sun. As instructed, they went through the rows picking out the ragwort so as not to poison animals by mixing it with the hay. They borrowed ancient rakes with huge wooden teeth. When they had drawn up the rows into haycocks, they leaned against them, like peasants in a painting, although they found the experience more prickly than picturesque.

The shaved grass bleached to a desert yellow in the sun and gradually turned green over the next few weeks, in time for the football season. Using the lawnmower, they manicured the larger space into stripes. Then, they looked out from their cottage. It was, for a while, as if the long meadow richness had never been there.

ROMANTICALLY REAL

So I've got past the fairy tale,
not waiting for my handsome prince
to save me.
No, I've saved myself
and I'm just waiting.
But still I want to shout
"Save me, save me!

Save me from the mind-numbing maths,
the daily doughnuts
leading to slimming sit-ups
and the sameness of it all.
Save me from the dinner-
and-dishes domestics,
the bitter backstabbing
and the wicked weekly night
of alcohol abuse.

Take me away
from the tit-for-tat backchat,
the daily searches for umbrellas
and foolish flings
with foolish fellas.
Lift me from this littleness!
Love away my loneliness.

Know me now
and understand me later.

An everyday love is what I'm after,
to put a shine on the littleness
and encourage laughter,
to be romantically real,
to make me feel that
I'm the lovely lady of the lemma,
the queen of theorems.
To wear an umbrella tiara
that glows gold when he says
'I love you'.

Siún McMorrow

ARE YOU THE ONE?

Clare Lynch

Are you the one who used to keep me up at nights? Sometimes your head invading my pillow...

Dreamlike or not, I used to imagine our conversations. How we would giggle and share together, then grow silent, electricity of fingers touching, the sigh, ahhhhhhhh.

In the morning you weren't there. Just reality. Jug kettles and alarm clocks and having to be certain places for certain times.

Where are you, now that you no longer visit my head? Are you in someone else's, captive of their thoughts and desires for you?

It was such a long time ago when we met first. Oh, I can't remember that meeting, let's be honest. It's when I gradually became aware of you, that's what I remember.

You were my Aran boy.

You were, hmmmmn, ten, maybe eleven. Do you remember it yourself? That stiff white Aran jumper that you used to wear?

Your mother was from Galway, if I recall correctly, and, for some reason, I seem to think she knitted it for you. People said she was great with her hands. I don't know about anything else but I remember the sweater.

Why is it I remember these things? I must've been just ten years old when I was hearing all that and yet that's the kind of thing I hold on to. I am a mental magpie, hoarding the useless, shiny pieces of gossip for my memory nest.

Anything to do with you was important to me. I picked up everything. If your father had met mine in town, if your family had bought a new car, if your parents were in O'Flynn's on Saturday night.

They were a great pair for the waltzing, my mother said. Do they still?

You sat before me in sixth class. I could read the boredom in your back in history class, your shoulder sloping to the left as you drove holes in the desk with your compass. Man Utd. I checked later. I was so desperate to know, to share that too.

The master never caught you. But I don't think you would have cared if he had. You were one of the enchanted ones. Born to float by, it seemed. I never saw you study or take a test seriously. The rest of us were biting our nails up to our elbows in dread. The master was so down on anyone who failed. Especially Irish.

No, I'm serious about this, I never saw you study or copy or get out of kilter in any way. Yet your name was always in the top three. Up on the board, again.

Me, for all my work, I may have scraped in tenth in a class of thirty.

But I was never jealous of you for that. In a way, you were my God;

my work was the sacrifice I willingly made to keep you where you deserved to be. I don't know. It was childish logic. I can't fit into it now; it's like clothes that I can't get into any more.

I loved your smile. It was like sun after showers somehow. Oh, how corny that seems but how true for you. Your skin was delightfully brown, even in the depths of January when we were sucking icicles off our anorak sleeves in the schoolyard. Raven black hair, just that enticing bit over your right eye that hid half of what you were thinking. All the rest of the lads gathered around you in that imitation manly huddle, practising for the day when you would all be old men, gathering outside the church gate, scuffling your shoes and kicking gossip like stones.

Yes. It was your smile. I'm convinced that's what made me see you.

There were other fellows with dark faces but they never drew me. Liam Reilly was one, as brown as a nut. But he was a sickener. His mouth was like a twisted clothes hanger and I know he spat on my sleeve once when I was passing him. A big globby spit. I nearly got sick when I went into the girls' cloakroom to clean it off, all green and sticky.

No, it was not the tanned skin.

Black hair, brown eyes, slow, easy smiles.

You set a blueprint in my heart that I have remained true to ever since. And somehow the whiteness of that Aran jumper made you heroic, on top of everything else. You were pure, unsullied. The other boys spat and cursed and pulled the girls' hair. You didn't. You held the door open without being a sissy. You held it open for me once when I was coming in off the Knockbride bus. I nearly died. One of my plaits was coming loose and my socks were at half-mast, all wrinkly and horrid. I sat at my desk and blushed for ages afterwards. Thank God you didn't look around. I was radioactive.

It was the first time I knew that my heart could sing – the time I had my crush on you.

You smelt of fresh soap like Palmolive or Shield. In every way you seemed freshly scrubbed, your face open to each new day. Your trousers always had a crease, razor-sharp, no chewing gum stains on the knees like the rest.

I thought all things would be all right in the world as long as you were. If there came a day when you were not at school, your empty chair was like a gravestone in front of me. I would not learn anything that day, took nothing in. There was no point. But the days when you had to turn around to borrow a ruler or to collect my copy with the grammar homework, oh, those were high points. Those were the days when my stars were in the ascendant. I was unbeatable, I was the beautiful Aphrodite…

There was nothing I wouldn't save you from in my daydreams. Dragons, fires, car crashes, house explosions – somehow I had the means to find you through it all and bring you safely home. It was chivalry all the way. I was chaste, full of integrity and courage – maybe a little bit sooty or suffering a glamorous cut here and there but nothing that would make me ugly. You were ever the grateful gentleman, always the perfect victim to rescue, with enough of your wits about you to know just how marvellous and brave I was, and all those good manners to express it.

Oh but why, why couldn't I ever talk to you?

Then came a day... Do you remember? The master wanted to know did any of us think we had a vocation? Did any of our parents tell us about the importance of passing on The Faith?

Did any of us want to be nuns or priests or brothers?

Hands up now, hands up now, who does...

Lámha suas, a pháisti...

I almost died, waiting in agony, afraid that you might raise yours.

You didn't.

I breathed again.

We sat like good children while the master talked about the future and whether we'd go on to the community or the vocational school. He wanted another 'hands up'. Vocational school?

Lámha suas, a pháisti...

You put up yours.

My heart nearly broke in two. I knew that my parents were sending me to the community school because it was closer and the pupils there didn't have to wear a uniform. My parents' cheapness was going to make me lose you. I hated them irrevocably. I wished nasty deaths upon them. Plagues, strokes, everything.

Surely I would never meet anyone else as pure as you at the community school. Dumb old community school. All the roughs went there, the corner boys from Ballinfull. There would be no one who spoke in the same soft, hesitant but considered way that you did, eyelashes lying like dark bristles against your cheek when you lowered your head to read your perfect answer from your copy.

But we didn't really understand about your sister Maeve. She was only little, in baby infants in Mrs Brady's class. She was smaller than the other children and wasn't well. That was all we knew. Then, one day, you weren't at school and the master was twenty minutes late calling out the roll because he had been in deep conversation with Mrs Brady and the other two teachers out in the yard.

When he came in, it took him a while to clear his throat. He said we all had to stand up and say an Our Father and three Hail Marys for Ciaran's sister, who died early that morning.

Poor little Maeve. What was she, five?

I tried to recall her frail bones, like a bird; the way you held her hand when you walked with her to the bus after school. She was only half the size of you, pale as porcelain, her tiny Mickey Mouse mitten clutched in your brown hand.

I couldn't find a way to get my prayer through the lump in my throat. All that day, it sat wedged there like gristle, the fingers of all my thoughts nearly choking my emotions to death. When I dragged in the door of home that afternoon, my mother was flying out to the car, her 'busy, busy, busy' voice on as she told me that I'd have to feed Major and make sure to shut in the hens before six.

She had the bag that she always brought to people's houses for laying out the dead. It seemed to be about cotton wool a lot of the time. I thought laying out dead people was all about making them comfortable, white and pure. She said to me once that I'd know more about it when I was older, but that was not what it was all about.

She came back three hours later and collapsed into the leatherette armchair. It wasn't like I was really interested in *Starsky and Hutch* that evening, so I heard all the hushed words between her and my father.

"That family is destroyed," was the bit I remember; her saying it over and over again, her head shaking over and back like a towel on a clothes line.

"That poor family... oh, she was like a baby angel, poor wee thing, her hair like a curly halo round her head, her wee toy rabbit in her arms. It'd bring tears to a stone, so it would. Poor little Ciaran, sure he doesn't understand. Crying his young heart out. Sure what would he know?"

I thought to myself. Ciaran's not little. He's twelve.

The master said we were to have black shoes on us for Wednesday and make sure they were polished. All of Ciaran's class were going up to the chapel for the funeral. He said how we would be a guard of honour, with all the girls on one side and all the boys on the other side of the chapel lane.

"If I see any nonsense, whoever's at the doin' of it will be thrown out of this school and not be let back," he said. But we knew why he was crotchety and we didn't laugh at him behind his back the way we usually would.

But not even Liam Reilly was in the mood for nonsense the next day. We had never seen a small, white coffin before. Some of us had been at our grandparents' funerals, with the big brown coffins blocking off the altar. But Maeve's coffin was just like a carry-cot, a doll gone to sleep for the last time.

The chapel was packed and I could not see you as all of us in sixth class kept quiet down at the back. There were tears and coughing sobs all the time. The Stations of the Cross hung over our heads like ominous sentinels, Christ scourging, Christ fallen, Christ dead. It all seemed real for the first time. I could feel my heart thudding in my chest. This was a horrible place to be. I would have preferred even rotten old geography. I didn't know what grown-up sadness was supposed to feel like and, even though all the grown-ups were crying, I knew no one there was sadder than me.

We stood all the way down the lane, lining it from the angry March wind that rattled the whin bushes behind our backs. The procession came out past us. The shuffle of steps on gravel. The priest's *ominy nominy* dull prayers as he cranked holy water over the little box, sad-faced altar boys like two big, frothy, white lampshades on either side of him, vestments blowing like gaudy white tablecloths. The squeezed eyes of your father's face as he carried the coffin with your uncle from Galway. Arms through arms, shuddering. Your mother being half-dragged, half-carried after the coffin by two women, her face an open scream of grief. I could hear her toes scraping the gravel. Everyone dressed in black or blue with red noses, white cheeks.

And you, another uncle's arm around you, you carried the long, red rose.

Sixth class stood the way the master told us to stand. We held our hands down by our sides and looked straight ahead. I was near the pillars because I was one of the tallest. My heart broke for you, tiny pieces of pain falling in chips on the gravel as you came nearer to where I was. There was never such emptiness before. For some reason you lifted your head as you came past me.

There was a look between us, the longest one ever.

I had never stared at anyone before and I never had intended to stare at you. Always been too afraid you'd catch me. But this was something I couldn't help. I was too sad to be afraid.

We caught each other's eye at the same time. I don't know how long that look lasted. It was beyond something that could be counted.

And then you were gone.

My eyes on the gravel again, looking for the pieces of my heart. I never, ever, felt so sad before. But more than the funeral sadness. It was the look in your brown eyes, stark with pain and tears, that told me that, somehow, you were already so much older than me and that we would never, ever talk.

OVERHEARD

Standing in the dim light of the bathroom,

I rub 1% hydrocortisone cream

into my re-emerging eczema;

dusty red trails of dry skin,

made shiny by ointment.

I can hear you on the phone in our bedroom next door,

sometimes muffled, sometimes clear,

to your sister in England;

the conspiratorial tones of siblings.

Should I listen or pretend not to?

The words come in and out of focus

like a badly-tuned radio,

though the tone and delivery seem unambiguous:

sarcastic, disdainful, touched with contempt,

not your usual style: measured, implacable.

This is a withering arctic wind

mercilessly turning extremities

into black-stumped apologies

of their former selves.

Then I catch my name.

It sounds like someone else's,

or rather, the words around it do:
cold and sharp and loveless,
like a knife slitting a pig's throat:
Dead before it squeals.

I hover around the closed door,
like a fly circling shit.
Oblivious behind it,
you rant about someone
unrecognisable to me,
someone wretched beyond forgiving:
a big joke
that isn't funny.

Seán Denyer

THE BIG FREEZE

Julia Stygall

It was the day after Christmas in 1962. I was six years of age and entranced by the whole prospect of going to see horses, with riders drinking port, and pretty ponies for me to pat.

My aged grandparents had come to join us for the festive season, decamping from their Yorkshire home to spend a few days in the Cotswolds. It was decided to take them with us 'for a spin in the car' – largely to alleviate the boredom we were all silently experiencing.

In the crisp morning, we went to see the foxhounds meet in the local market town. My grandmother was done up to the nines in her lace bodice, navy-blue suit, court shoes and the obligatory hat. Grandfather was wearing his special, grey business suit and dark tie for the occasion. I wondered why they stayed in the car.

On our way home, the world outside began its transformation, a cunning trick to show us that nature was still in charge.

My grandfather – a man of few words in times of crisis or elation – was particularly quiet. I noticed his demeanour very early on in our short journey. Anxious of eye, he was peering upwards, out of the window. I jumped at the sound of his voice from the back seat: "The sky's a funny colour and, by the way, I think you've got a puncture."

My father pulled gently onto the verge and confirmed Grandad's suspicions – flat tyre and snow coming. Still wearing her summer hat and with her arms crossed, my grandmother remained seated: "William, get out and do something about this".

I remained silent, as something magical was happening. A frozen lump of rain hit the windscreen and the gathering wind brought showers of similar little bodies, hurrying across the green valley in a dancing cloud, like an anxious crowd gravitating towards a desirable venue.

In seconds, the windscreen was covered by a white coating and I looked round to gauge the reactions of my grandparents. There was silence – backed by expressions of dread. I later discovered that they were both thinking the same thoughts: they were already sufficiently bored by our rural life that the journey home to Yorkshire was the best thing on their horizon. Now that horizon had disappeared in a matter of minutes.

When my father cleared the windscreen with his arm, we saw his face grinning in at us, or was it grimacing, his hair topped with hail?

"Not to worry," he reassured. "We'll be on the move again in a minute or two." He was right, this far.

Five minutes after changing the tyre, we ground to a halt again, as the wind had deposited a thick blanket of snow onto the lowest part of the road home. It was decided to stop the car, before we became completely stuck.

Next, we had to persuade Grandma to get out. My father generously donated his Wellingtons boots, so that she could have at least a chance of being well equipped to start the two-mile walk home.

Urgency was not a word that appeared in my grandparents' vocabulary. Much muttering ensued but we set off into the swirling greyness towards our cottage.

"Daddy, it's not that way," I said.

"Darling, just come along with me."

After a few minutes, we realised we were no longer on the road – we were in a field. A local farmer was attempting to encourage a few bewildered sheep to move towards higher ground.

The farmer quickly spotted that we were actually heading away from civilisation and cheerily offered Grandma a lift on his tractor, assuring us that he would come back for us directly, when he had deposited his precious cargo. One by one, we were all delivered home.

For three weeks, the village was cut off by road, with only tinned food from the local shop to sustain us, and the grandparents still, silently, in place.

The dry-stone walls around our garden had been transformed into alpine slopes as the snow drifts banked up and above them. The same farmer took me out with him on the tractor, to "see something you may never see the like of again".

Gingerly alighting, he scraped the snow and revealed a piece of round wood.

"It's the top of a telegraph pole."

I was duly amazed, and trust to this day it really was!

The greatest excitement for seemingly ages came in the form of a helicopter from Oxford airport, bringing papers from my father's office for him to work on: deadlines wouldn't wait for the thaw. With no telephone and no chance of escaping, the 'chopper' was the solution; at least he could make a start. It hovered, causing the grandparents to become surprisingly vocal; a small smile passed between them.

When the package dropped onto our white lawn, we realised that business wheels were turning, while the real ones were still locked in immobility, as dictated by the elements, which for ever would be superior.

My grandparents just had to remain quiet and wait for nature to smile upon them. It did, after three long, baked-bean-filled weeks. Christmas was spent without them from then on. I shall never understand quite why.

OYSTER GIFT

He gave me a dustpan and brush for Valentine's Day,
in spite of many hints and harping
about how I needed a pair of ear-rings.

But this was indeed a gift of love,
a thoughtful gift.
The dustpan had a long handle,

so I didn't have to bend
to gather dust;
it was green to match my kitchen colour

and was needed because
my old one was broken.
When making our Valentine's dinner,

I stirred in love with the pasta,
trust with the salmon,
friendship with the sauce,

and longing with every oyster,
which, when opened, yielded up
my pearl ear-rings as well.

Paula Daly

OUMA FOO (from *Kathy's Ghost*)

Michael Clement

One day his mother left George alone with Ouma Foo. The old woman said: "Go, Elsie. I will look after the boy."

The man at the store called her Miss Bloem to her face when she came in to buy her groceries. But behind her back he referred to her as the strange old woman who always wore black. He was not sure if he cared for her much. Ouma Foo did not care for the man at the store. She did not care for any man. In her sixty-three years of life, she had never felt or desired the caress of a man. Once when Herbert, her brother-in-law, had frivolously tried to tickle her, she recoiled in disgust and his hand had accidentally brushed against one of her breasts.

"Don't you dare!" she spat, glaring at him. "No man will ever touch me there!"

Now inside the old, dark cottage, she sat brooding, cradling her secret wound deep within the folds of her black Victorian dress. Outside, the cottage was surrounded by a veranda to shade the occupants from the blistering African sun. In the dusty distance, an acacia tree shimmered in the Transvaal heat. Beyond the barbed wire fence, a skeletal thorn bush stood transfixed, crucified by the heat. A lone kestrel circled high in the turquoise sky, eyeing the terrain for carrion. The blood-red, corrugated-iron roof sheet crackled and buckled in the heat. The clean shimmering air was loud with the indolent buzzing of flies and the distant laugh of the young farm boys splashing and dancing half-naked at the water pump, clicking their Xhosa tongues. The fly-screen door to the kitchen squealed and clattered in its green wooden frame every time it was opened. From inside the kitchen, the smell of boiled cabbage and strong coffee wafted. There was the dull clatter of an aluminium pot. Cynthia, the big-bottomed woman in the white apron, stood at the ceramic sink, singing Xhosa praises to Jesus. *Inkosa Sikelele Afrika.*

In the living-room, away from the linoleum-floored kitchen, the dark wooden floorboards gleamed with polish. The silence was punctuated by the hollow ticking of the hall clock. Ball and claw dressers stood sullenly against the walls of the room, listening to the determined tick-tick-tick. On the embroidered couch sat Ouma Foo with a gleaming needle, picking at a piece of strangled lace. Numerous layers of rustling starched petticoats, black lace and cloth veiled her womanhood. No breast, thigh or hip was visible.

She sat with lips pursed, austere, neck held stiffly. Dignified, she carried the aloofness of purity. *God knows what is best for my children.* From beneath the voluminous petticoats her stocking-clad ankles peered. Her tiny feet were laced in black leather. She wore sensible shoes.

The boy sat at her feet on the rug, playing. The small white bones of the *dol osse*, the ox vertebrae, had become: first a wagon, then a dog, now a child. The carpet became a landscape, its threaded patterns coloured mountains, rivers and trees. The boy was barefoot; his feet were dusty and leathered like those of the black boys that were his playmates.

He rolled on the rug, in shorts and shirt, humming and growling and pushing the bone animals across the woven landscape. Then he paused and looked up at the dark mountain of Calvinist cloth and lace.

"Ouma, when is Ma coming home?"

Ouma Foo tightened her mouth and looked across the room at the clock. There were many hours still. There were still many hours to sit with the boy.

He gave a squeal of delight. She glared at him.

"Be quiet!"

He shrank back in terror. He knew her eyes. It had been many hours now. The day had been too long for both of them. George gathered up the small white bones and slipped them into his pocket. He rolled off the mat and slid his bottom over the polished wooden floor until he was beneath the towering dresser. The ball and claw feet embraced him darkly with their shadow.

The old woman glared icily at the boy for a moment and then reached for the scissors that lay on the cushion beside her. The back of her thumb and knuckles levered away the black cast-iron handles and the blades flashed open in a promise of sharp steel. Shlink. Shlink. They sliced mercilessly through the yielding white cloth.

Thump. The boy bumped up against the underside of the dresser with his back. There was a brief clink and tinkle. The china plates trembled in their wire stands. The old woman's dark eyes flashed like ravens' beaks at the boy. The gnarled fist curled tightly around the pair of scissors. The opened mouth formed by the gaping blades snapped together to form a single gleaming point. A dagger.

The boy's clear eyes darted to the old hand, to the cold steel scissors. He gasped, drawing in a small breath. His body tightened and jerked beneath the solid body of the Imbue dresser. His back straightened and his one shoulder pushed up against the underside of the drawer. The dresser rocked. The large, white plate with the faded blue pattern, Ouma Foo's special plate, rocked, trembled, and then pitched forward. Silently it free-fell for a second and then struck the wooden floor. It exploded, smashing, fragmenting, scattering chunks of jagged white porcelain like shattered bone across the dark, gleaming floor.

The old woman's nostrils flared beneath her hooked nose. She sprang to her feet. The delicate cloth fell, crumpling on the floor. Her right hand still grasped the scissors. She strode to the dresser. Her left hand darted down and clutched at the boy, finding shirt, finding hair. She dragged him out. The left hand clawed at his neck. He screamed.

"No!"

Her face bent down close to his face as she thrust the scissors toward his small pale throat, bobbing, swallowing. Her dry lizard lips curled and parted to reveal her clenched yellow teeth, yellow teeth like filthy fragments of crushed corn.

"Do you want me to stab you, boy?"

The boy paled as the hand clawed once again at the straws of his hair and bent back his head.

"No." His voice was weaker this time, almost choking.

A small wet patch appeared on the front of his khaki shorts and pale yellow liquid trickled down his dusty leg, pooling on the glistening, wooden floor.

The old woman sniffed, then she peered down past her black skirts onto the floor. Her mouth turned down sourly.

"You little pig!"

She released her grip on his neck for a moment, and then clawed his fair hair tightly in her hand, a hand blotched with brown stains and furrowed with tortured veins that snaked across the back like serpents twisting between the roots of dead trees.

Ouma Foo dragged the flailing boy across the sitting-room floor, her eyes now fixed on the door of the bedroom, half ajar. She pushed her way through, the door yielding willingly. She dragged him into the tiny bedroom, the bedroom with its small window looking out onto the sunlit yard, the horse pen and the distant pump.

The room was furnished with a high bed and a wooden cupboard.

"Little pig! I'll teach you a lesson."

She dragged the boy across the floor. He screamed weakly between breaths. His bare heels dragged a smudge of damp urine across the immaculately polished floor. His eyes were wild with fear. The gnarled hand still grasped the scissors as she twisted open the cupboard.

"Get in there or I'll stab you!" she hissed, forcing the child into the darkness of the cupboard. Quickly she slammed the door shut, and turned the fretted-silver key in the lock. The boy's screams were muffled now and the cupboard rocked slightly with his struggles, the frantic thudding of fist and foot against wood. Still the odour of urine and now the faint sharpness of excrement.

The old woman looked up for a moment into the quivering mirror on the cupboard door. She stared into the alien face for a moment and then snarled back at the apparition that confronted her. Clutching at the key, she pulled it from the lock and thrust it deep into the folds of her dark petticoats. She turned with a look of disgust and stalked from the room. Ouma Foo, the old woman in black, slammed the door behind her. She could no longer hear the banging and screaming.

VAPORETTO

Handsome gondoliers
serenade us through
blue lagoons
toward piazzas
teeming with
doves and dukes.

High church spires,
pealing bells,
invite us to
observe
ornate buildings,
or behold them
mirrored in
Venetian waters.

Sonorous sounds
waft across the bay
to bid us stay
another day.

Mary Gallagher

HER FATHER'S GHOST

Mary Molloy

The gentle African breeze fanned her hair and caressed her body through the transparency of her green chiffon dress. Nairobi airport was scorching. She clutched her large handbag close to her, its leather burning the tanned skin of her arm. It was good to be back in Africa after such a long absence. She felt her heart pounding and her blood was burning higher. Her old wanderlust had returned. But this time she had come back to the land of her birth with a mission. Her father's ghost haunted her. She had come to bury that ghost.

She boarded the train that would take her into the heart of Kenya. She could already smell the blossoms, she could almost hear the throbbing echo of the lion's roar. The stars were mellow and large in the dark African sky as she stepped off the train into the town that had been her home for so many years. The keen, cool rush of the night air was refreshing. The ghost must be buried. Tomorrow she would do it in the crisp, clean dawn. She would scatter her father's ashes over Mount Kenya, the mountain that was so dear to his heart.

A taxi stopped for her, ignoring a Kikuyu woman and her child. She ushered him on. Beth observed the soiled, sorry band of street urchins trying to elicit sympathy. She carried on up the street to the garage where she hired a car.

She thought of her father, a highly successful lawyer. Oxford educated, Anton Blake had come over from Britain at the time of Kenyan independence to help in the transfer of power. Kenya offered the prospect of Eden. He fell in love with the country and stayed. His wife, Laura, was a non-practising nurse and they were married shortly before they arrived in Kenya. *Uhuru* was the cry of all Kenyans then: *Uhuru* meant freedom, independence, Nirvana.

Beth was their only child. Beautiful and spoilt, with the face of a Botticelli angel, her voice rang of money. Academically gifted like her father, she also had an artistic flair, which she decided to further, much to the annoyance of her ultra-conservative father. Headstrong and self-willed, she decided to pay her way through art college by posing as an artist's model. She thought about her father now. He was her sparring partner as her mother so often had said. Yet there had been warmth and camaraderie and humour between them despite the underlying tensions and disagreements.

How different the situation had been since her mother's death. The morbidity of the last two years made her shiver involuntarily. His antagonism since Laura's death had turned to open antipathy despite her best efforts to care for him. They had both returned to his birthplace in the Lake District after her mother's death.

They lived there for two years until the insidious cancer that gnawed away at his intestines resulted in his death. He became cantankerous and hard to live with and there was never any real reconciliation between them.

During the trip her mood swung widely. She though of Jeff. Their marriage was now a sham. She remembered the good times. Jeff was born of an American father and a Kikuyu mother. His bronze skin gleamed in the summer sun. She remembered their first date. His eyes burned like topaz in the dark African night as he held and kissed her tenderly. And now he was gone. They were all gone. Everyone she had ever loved. Her parents had been aghast at the relationship but she had been determined to marry him and she had. He was a highly regarded professional photographer. They had travelled the world together, he taking photographs of wild life for *National Geographic* and Beth doing her marvellous oil paintings of the lions, the elephants, the zebras and all the profusion of wildlife across the hemispheres. Their life seemed idyllic, one endless saga of bliss and fulfilment. She remembered the painting for which she had won the award. It was a beautiful picture – the spotted coat of the big, lithe, formidable cat fairly shone as it snarled defiance. There was nothing tentative here about her brush strokes, they were bold, provocative.

She found him in bed one night with Kina, the Kikuyu woman. She felt nothing but revulsion and never wanted to see him again. Now, Beth thought, if she could see his face one more time, talk to him the way they used to talk…

As she drove to Mount Kenya the goats champed and jumped. Big white clouds hung over the mountain. The sweet breath of flowers washed through the breeze. At the foot of the mountain she opened the large leather bag with the bronze urn. She then made her decisive gesture. She flung the ashes far and wide and said a little prayer. Her spirituality was important to her. It gave her a sense of purpose, belonging. Jeff cared little for religion. His was a wild pantheism that saw the rugged landscape and wildlife as being a god in themselves. She thought of the happy wonderful days she and Jeff had spent together. She felt an irresistible urge to see him again. She knew his hideaway was not far away. Yes! She would visit him one more time. Decisively she turned the car around. She put her foot firmly on the accelerator and she was away. She could feel her heart throbbing with anticipation. She was going extremely fast now, ninety-five miles an hour. Suddenly a gazelle appeared from nowhere. Aghast at the thought of killing such a wonderful creature, she swerved immediately. The car hit a boulder and somersaulted. She knew no more.

Jeff and Kina were driving along in their jeep at a leisurely pace. He was looking for some good shots and Kina, with her olive skin and dark eyes, was just admiring the general scenery. Suddenly a wrecked car caught Jeff's eye. He drove swiftly in its direction, jumped from his jeep to view the wreck and saw Beth's bloodstained body. Kina, a qualified nurse, realised that she was still alive but needed urgent surgery. An ambulance was out of the question in this wild terrain. Gently they lifted Beth into the jeep and with great haste rushed to the hospital in Embu. She was operated on immediately for a ruptured spleen, and the prognosis was bleak. She badly needed blood and hers was a very rare blood group. The consultant was helpful but not optimistic about finding a blood match in time.

Suddenly Kina blurted out: "I could be the perfect match."

"What makes you think that?" said Jeff.

"Because I'm her half-sister," replied Kina. "Her father was my father too. He never acknowledged me, but Anton Blake had an affair with my mother shortly after he got married and I was the result. I'm willing to do anything I can to help."

A blood sample was taken immediately and, as luck would have it, it turned out to be a match. A successful blood transfusion was performed, and then the patient was pronounced stable. Beth made a slow but sure recovery in the days that followed. She was showered with flowers, gifts, and cards from her many friends and well-wishers in Embu. Jeff and Kina thought they should keep the identity of the donor a secret, at least until Beth was feeling ready to hear the news. However, an indiscreet and malicious young nurse blurted out the whole story to her. Beth was incredulous. She simply didn't, couldn't, believe that her ultra-conservative father could have fathered a child out of wedlock, especially as he had only been married two years. She consulted Jeff.

"It's true," he told her. "The evidence is there in the DNA."

She was aghast. Her father had been so racially superior that he had objected to her marrying a coloured man while he himself fathered a child by an African woman. And Kina was the result.

"Kina saved your life, she didn't have to spill the beans," said Jeff.

"I know and I'm extremely grateful," Beth replied. "We're sisters now so I suppose we should be friends. Send her in. I want to see her. I want to thank her."

Beth and Kina gave one another an embrace. The two arch-enemies were at last reconciled. However, Beth had much reconciling to do in her own heart.

She realised now that she had come to Africa to bury her father's ghost in more senses than one. There was a skeleton in the cupboard that would have utterly devastated her mother if she had known.

"Thank God she died before she knew," thought Beth. The next day Beth boarded the plane that would take her out of Africa, what Conrad had called the "Heart of Darkness", for ever. Unremittingly for ever.

TRANSIENCE

The moss-covered stone pathway
gleaming from the soft rain
of a late August day
leads me.

The half-shut rust-coated gate
dancing with the devil while
the sun chases the rain
beckons me.

The overhanging sycamores
a rainbow arch of green
spitting drops in a breeze
teases me.

The dank unkempt undergrowth
strangling the life spirit
sprouting from earth
draws me

to this wasteland of silence
through a cold eerie air
of another place to
show me

an old gravestone by the wall
with a name inscribed and
uncovered by time…
It's me.

Paddy Donoghue

A GREAT TEAM

Paula Daly

The parrot, her exotic plumage fluffed up in anger, hopped agitatedly from claw to claw.

"Yea, yea, cackle, cackle, yack, yack," muttered the hedgehog under his breath, making a fairly good impression of parrot sounds. "Yes, not bad," he thought to himself, as he had been practising all week, but now the parrot had flown in, thinking it was another parrot calling to him, and had discovered his trick.

"Are you mimicking me? Are you mimicking me?" she spat.

Hedgehog called back, louder this time: "Are you mimicking me? I am mimicking you, moron!"

At this insult, the parrot swooped down to attack, but not fast enough, as the hedgehog had quickly rolled himself into a prickly ball. The parrot retreated to the branch, nursing a wounded claw. Silence reigned for a few minutes.

"Have you calmed down yet?" a muffled voice came from the centre of the prickly ball, "because I have a proposition to make".

Parrots, being curious birds by nature – and this one was no exception – lifted her head from the task of preening her wound and said: "What proposition?" Whereupon the hedgehog unravelled himself, shook out his spines and settled himself once more under the tree.

"Are you looking at me?" squawked the parrot, her hackles rising. "Calm down, bird, you're giving me migraine," replied the hedgehog, scratching at the soft spot on his underbelly. "I'm getting too old for all this rolling up in a ball stuff, I need a quiet life, so will we call a truce, or what?"

"Or what, or what, or what?" began the parrot again, but suddenly, she became very still and very quiet, as the shadow of something bigger than both of them darkened the sky above. Suddenly, a big net was thrown over the two of them and, before they knew it, they were in the back of a truck on the way to the market town of Anganiki.

"Bird," said the hedgehog quietly, "we have to work together on this one, or I am soup and you are a feather duster, so listen to me now and do what I say". And so they hatched a plan, and the parrot pecked and the hedgehog prickled and soon they had a fair-sized hole in the net.

"Now," said hedgehog, "I'll roll into a ball, you grab me in your claws, and fly up. When you get above the driver's head, drop me on his head and I'll do the rest, OK?"

"OK," squeaked a very scared parrot and, grabbing the hedgehog as instructed, she flew up out of the net, screeching loudly, and dropped the hedgehog on the driver's head. The spines went into the driver's eye and into his ear and into his head and he was in such a state that he drove the truck into a tree, jumped out and ran for his life!

"Nice work, bird," said the hedgehog.

"Nice work, hedgehog," said the parrot, and they never fought over anything again.

SWEET SIX-TINA

I

I tried to sing a song of six
Six simple lines in every verse
Six simple verses in each song
Six simple words at each line's end
And in the next six, working back
Reversing order in six ways.

II

I set the song in different ways
Still keeping to the rule of six
And in the next verse back to back
I set the order in <u>re</u> verse
And thought that it would never end
This complicated sixy song.

III

Now if I want to sing a song
With six words ordered different ways
And each repeated at line's end
I have to choose a useful six
words, crafted well in every verse
Or else my song will be sent back.

IV

If someone sends my poor song back
And says it is a silly song

In spite of six lines to a verse

and six words ordered in six ways,

I'll try another song of six

And persevere until the end.

V

Rejection cannot be the end

I will rewrite and send it back

Six times and thirty-six times six

Until they learn to sing my song

And start to think in six new ways

To know and love my complex verse.

VI

I've got as far as the sixth verse

With one of six words at line's end

And used them all in six neat ways

Six lines, six verses back to back

To make my pretty little song

A sweet sestina, song of six.

VII

Well, now this verse is at the back

So it can end my little song

And anyways that's more than six!

Órfhlaith Ní Chonaill

THE CONFRONTATION

Eileen Sheridan

The day Kate joined our class, she was introduced to us by Sr. Fidelma. We got the usual admonition to make her welcome, that it was difficult being new in the school, especially in the middle of the school year, and that it was our duty as Christian young ladies to welcome the stranger into our midst.

I watched Kate while all this was being said. She wasn't a very attractive girl in the physical sense. Her chest was still very flat, she was skinny and had slightly protruding teeth. She would be a great addition to the school, Sr. Fidelma added.

I was certain that Kate was already watching and waiting for her chance to show us all how smart she was. She didn't seem at all shy or nervous like I would have been if I had been in her position. I could see some of the other girls beaming at her as she basked in the glory of her novelty.

The next class was a double period of English and Sr. Alice was on top form. We listened intently as she read from *Macbeth* and then we responded enthusiastically to her questions. Kate remained silent during this class and the next one.

Miss Maguire was our maths teacher and had come new to the school at the beginning of the school year. Maths was my favourite subject and I wanted to find out as much as I could. Unfortunately, Miss Maguire appeared to be one of those teachers who kept but one chapter ahead of the class and, consequently, there were many times when she was unable to enlighten us. On these occasions she would rifle through her notes, look flustered and do her best to divert the questioner. We were used to this and, although it was annoying, we were more embarrassed at her lack of expertise than anything else. We had learned to accept the situation and to keep the more difficult questions to ourselves.

Five minutes into the class, Kate raised her hand and asked for an explanation of an algebraic formula. She had noticed, as had I, that Miss Maguire had glossed over it in the textbook. I looked over at Kate and saw that she was taking in the whole class as she spoke. Miss Maguire went into her usual routine. As her colour deepened, Kate's smile broadened.

"We don't need to go into that yet, girls," said Miss Maguire.

"But, Miss, I would really like to know it for later on."

"I must move on, Kate."

"It won't take you long to explain it, I'm sure, Miss. My father will probably ask what I'm doing in maths. He's really interested in maths, Miss. I'd like to be able to explain this formula to him."

"Let's see, ahm, well, ahm…"

Miss Maguire was beginning to perspire and there was a titter of laughter from near Kate's desk. She was making sure that she remained serious, but I could see the smirk on her face and the glint in her eye as she glanced around at those girls who were already her minions. I wanted so much to stand up and tell her to be quiet, but of course I did no such thing.

"Well, if you can't answer, I suppose I'll have to ask my father to explain it to me."

Miss Maguire turned towards the blackboard and the titters grew louder. She rubbed the eraser over the board for some minutes until she was in control again and then she continued. The rest of the class passed very slowly. Kate continued to interrupt with irrelevant questions and Miss Maguire stumbled through her answers to even the most trivial of Kate's queries. She dismissed us five minutes early with no homework to do.

I hated Kate at that moment and knew that this would be the pattern during our maths class from now on. She would do her best also to embarrass Sr. Peter, our Irish teacher, when she realised that her grasp of that language was far from fluent. I knew that these teachers would not report her to Sr. Fidelma because they were afraid of being seen as weak.

As Kate was one of the 'townies', she went home at lunch break for her dinner. The girls in our group, being too far from home, had to stay in school and eat from paper bags. We had got to know each other well and friendships that had formed in first year had lasted through the years. We were inclined to stick to our own group and so Kate treated us with uninterested disdain. We were glad not to have to put up with her during that break.

However, small break was a different matter. Kate hung around with her pals, eyeing each girl that passed and making comments and jokes at the expense of those who were likely targets. She never confronted us directly but we avoided her gaze and stayed away from her group. Kate had collected around her the five most troublesome girls in the class. As soon as she arrived she had courted them, seeking them out like radar and becoming their leader by the end of the first week. I watched her manipulate them and mould them until they were just as she wanted. The loud raucous laughter of her cronies grated on my nerves but I kept with my own friends and we scorned her company.

Bernie was not in our class. She was in the lowest academic stream, so we had no contact with her. She did not mix with her classmates either but, instead, stayed with her sisters in the schoolyard during break. They formed a little group of their own, the three of them. They came to school and went home together also. The Feeney girls stood out because they wore torn, dirty clothes, broken shoes, and often had no socks. Their hair was matted together due to lack of washing and brushing, and they had the appearance of children from the slums of forty years before. I often thought that they looked just like those pictures of the Dublin tenements in our history books. I felt sorry for Bernie, though. She was my age and her sisters were younger.

Kate started on Bernie as soon as she saw her standing in the schoolyard with her sisters.

"Well, if it isn't the Feeney gang?"

Bernie backed away silently from her.

"Couldn't find the hairbrush this morning, Bernie?"

Kate's friends giggled in the background.

"Ah well, it can happen to the best of us."

I watched and cringed as Kate got more and more insulting.

"What's for lunch? Smoked salmon sandwiches I'll bet. How about swapping lunches, Bernie?"

I wanted to say something, to tell her to stop and to leave them alone, but I just couldn't.

After Kate left, Bernie watched her without saying a word. I longed to comfort her but then, I had never spoken to her so what could I say?

On a freezing cold January day when we were just back to school after the Christmas break, we were waiting for our second class to begin. Our teacher was delayed for some reason and, as usual, we had converged on the radiators at the back of the classroom. Kate and her friends had the best positions, of course, and Kate was looking out the window into the yard.

"Oh, oh, here they come, heading for trouble. Must have spent too much time over breakfast this morning," she spoke sarcastically.

We all looked out at the three Feeneys who were walking into the schoolyard. Though it was freezing and there was frost still on the ground, they had no coats on, much less hats or gloves. Instead, they wore layers of old skirts and jumpers, and I could see from their pinched faces that they were cold to the bone. I shivered and was about to turn away when Kate spoke again.

"Oh God, there's Sr. Fidelma and her sidekick!"

There was silence in the room as we crowded around to see what was about to happen. The Feeneys were late; they had missed first class and were now in for a severe talking to. Even Kate stayed silent but, as the nuns approached Bernie and her sisters, she silently opened the window. The cold air rushed into the classroom. We stayed where we were.

Now Bernie had seen Sr. Fidelma and Sr. Consilio approaching and she stopped in the centre of the yard. Her sisters stopped behind her, bumping into each other as they did so. The nuns continued walking right up to the girls. I wanted to turn away and return to my desk but I could not tear my eyes away. Nor could any of us. We strained to see out the windows but not a word was spoken.

"Well, what does this mean, Miss Feeney?" roared Sr. Fidelma. "What time do you think it is? Answer me I tell you!"

There was no reply from Bernie. She stood silently with her head bowed. She waited for the nun to continue.

Sr. Fidelma reached out and pushed Bernie to one side. She grabbed one of the younger girls and pulled her forward. The child cowered before her.

"Answer me, you imbecile," she shouted at the child. "How dare you come into my school at this time! Who do you think you are? You ungrateful bunch of stupid children!"

Sr. Fidelma pushed the child out of her way and she fell to the ground. There was a collective gasp from the girls around me. I put my hands to my mouth in terror. Bernie had stepped in front of her sisters and was helping the little one to her feet.

"Leave her there," screamed Sr. Fidelma. "Do not move until I tell you to."

Bernie continued to help her sister who was sobbing noisily now. We saw, and heard at the same time, the blow to Bernie's head. She staggered back and I thought she would fall as well.

Kate suddenly pushed up the window as far as it would go. She thrust her head out and shouted as loudly as she could.

"Leave them alone, you bully," she roared as she waved her fist in the air. "Don't touch them again or you'll pay for it."

Three of the girls in the classroom slumped to the floor in terror at this and the rest of us watched Kate in terrified amazement. The nuns were looking up at the open window, at Kate standing there waving her fist and admonishing them for their actions.

I looked at Kate and for a moment she looked like a picture I had seen in my history book: Countess Markievicz addressing the crowds in Dublin. I pushed my way to Kate's side at the window and I leaned out alongside her. I wanted to be seen standing by her side.

She continued to shout at the nuns and they stood in the freezing yard saying nothing. I don't think they knew what to say.

The Feeney girls had turned and left the yard. Bernie walked with her arms around her sisters but she kept looking back at the window and at Kate and me standing there with the two nuns looking up at us in silence.

We waited all that day for the explosion to come, but classes continued as normal except that Kate was not her usual disruptive self. I caught her looking at me on a number of occasions but we did not speak.

All weekend I expected a call from Sr. Fidelma to my parents but none came. The next school day was Monday. The Feeneys returned to school as usual but there was no sign of Kate. Nobody mentioned her name – not even her so-called pals. We heard later that she had moved to a posh boarding school in the next county. I never met her again but occasionally I see her on television now. She appears on programmes with politicians debating the problems of injustice and poverty. She can still cut to the bone.

As for Bernie, I would like to say that we became friends after the yard incident but we were too unalike for that. However, when we came across each other in the yard after the confrontation we always smiled and said, 'hello'.

Nowadays, Bernie is a smart and well-dressed woman. I met her recently at a parents' meeting. It was on the subject of bullying.

"You know," she said, "sometimes it is better to be taunted and insulted than to be invisible."

MY FATHER LOVED PIGEONS

My father loved pigeons.
He kept them and bred them
ever since he was a child.

He built his own cages
from wooden packing cases,
black creosote poles
and silver wire mesh.

My father would spend hours
by the loft in our garden
sitting in a chair, smoking
and looking at his pigeons.

Then one day he gave away
all his precious pigeons
until he was the only pigeon
left all alone.

He dismantled his loft
dismembering
plank and pole and wire.

Then he perched
upon an apartment roof
and launched himself
into wingless flight.

Weary from too much flying
he fixed his navigating heart
upon the guiding stars
and let instinct and gravity
take him home.

Michael Clement

DO YOU KNOW WHAT I'M SAYING? (from Cicada)

John Cullen

A lot's happened in the last year, and when I tell you about it you'll understand why I've changed so much. Back then I lived at home with Mum, a sort of sheltered existence, as I said to the doctor. I told her a whole heap of things, stuff I'd had bottled up inside me for years, like how Dad left when I was really young, and about how Mum kept me on a tight rein.

Everyone helps their mum out, but with me it was abnormal. I told the doctor that the closest I got to playing with the other boys in the flats where I lived was watching them from my window playing football in the evenings after school and at weekends, on the grassy hill in front of our kitchen window. All sorts of boys – blacks, whites, Irish, Greeks – aged about twelve to twenty-four. Whenever Mum went out, to Mass or the shops, I would stand at the kitchen window and watch them, listening to their shouts and the thump of the rubber ball being kicked. Sometimes I got so engrossed in the game that my leg twitched as if to kick the ball. Do you know what I'm saying?

On the other side of the hill was a steep railway embankment that ran all the way down to the railway tracks about a hundred yards below. The embankment was covered mainly in long grass, bushes and briars but at the end, to my right as I looked out my window, there was a small wood where some of the kids used to play, even though that was trespassing on railway property. In the summer I couldn't see them, because of a row of tall trees in front of the concrete wall, but you could hear their shrill voices drifting faintly through the trees. Phil Dunne told me that, two years ago, he and three other boys built a tree-house about ten foot up a tree, using nails and pieces of wood that the workmen had left behind. Phil lives in the flats too. He's my mate, a diamond geezer. We got to know each other last year through travelling together to school on the train.

I'll tell you more about him later. One of the boys who helped build the tree-house was this black kid nicknamed 'Moonhead' on account of his domey forehead. When it was finished he went and fetched cooked sausages wrapped in tin foil for the others to eat. Phil said they were the best sausages he'd ever tasted. They used the tree-house as a hiding place that summer and once, when the Old Bill came to the flats after a newsagent's was raided, they hid out over there for half a day.

They made the tree-house rainproof by nailing plastic sheeting over the roof. Phil said that he went there a few times by himself, after his dad came home drunk and started shouting and arguing with his mum. He even brought a blanket and stayed there one night during a particularly bad row. Phil and the others have been playing over the railway since they were small kids. He told me how they used to make bows and arrows and play cowboys and Indians. He got into trouble once at primary school after taking a cowboy's badge from a box of toys that had been collected for an orphanage.

Phil also told me that he and Charlie, his Nigerian next door neighbour, collected a jar full of grasshoppers over the railway, then tipped them through the letterbox of the local library. The next day he went in there pretending to look for a book, and the place was infested with grasshoppers. Another occasion that he found highly amusing recounting to me was when he and Charlie sneaked out one night with a pair of binoculars, and spied on the backs of the houses on the other side of the railway track. He swears they watched a woman getting undressed and even a couple having sex standing up. Both of them got really excited and nearly ended up fighting over the binoculars. That was the first time he remembers getting an erection, he claimed, but he didn't tell Charlie.

Phil mentioned the toboggan run they made over the embankment last year, which I remember because it was directly in front of my window. They found a roll of that green, plastic-covered mesh fence – the kind they used to have around school playgrounds – that had been taken down and replaced by a concrete wall, and they unrolled it down the slope, pegged it down with sticks and placed some old mattresses at the bottom. Then they used a plastic bread crate as a toboggan, and took it in turns to whiz down it. At one point nearly every kid in the flats was over there having a go, except me of course. I haven't told Phil this, but Mum phoned up the council to inform them that somebody was going to get hurt or killed. The next day the caretaker went over and dismantled it.

In the winter the kids would make a slide by throwing water down one of the steep walkways and waiting for it to freeze. It's amazing how imaginative children can be. It's a shame I missed out on all those kind of things, but Mum wouldn't let me mix with the other kids because they were a 'bad influence', as she put it.

If she ever caught me watching the boys she scolded me.

"What are you watching them for, they're only a rabble. I don't want you mixing with the likes of them, you're better than that. You're going to do something with your life."

That's how it started usually, how I was going to be an officer in the armed forces but that I needed a degree first, which meant I had to do extremely well in my school exams. Ironic that, don't you think? Anyway, that's how the pressure started. She'd been going on like that for as long as I can remember, and this pressure to do well at school had been building up gradually over the years. But it wasn't until a few weeks before my 'O' Level exams were due that I began to really notice it. It felt as if my entire life, and Mum's, hinged on that couple of weeks, and those five or six papers with a few questions on them. Looking back on it now, I think that I got in a bit of a panic, and that's when I started getting confused.

It first happened one evening as I was revising equations. I've always been comfortable with equations, ever since I was first introduced to them a few years ago. But this particular night I was in my bedroom scribbling away when a noise from outside distracted me. A car was pulling into the car park beneath my window and music was blaring from its sound system. Normally the kind of music you heard in the flats was horrible: reggae or disco music. You get a lot of that around here. You see them driving along Green Lane in these flash cars with the windows wound down and the music blaring really loudly so that the car is like a mobile disco. In the flats there were two or three that played really loud music all the time. Why do they have to turn it up so loud? You could tell they

Dolly Mixtures

turned it up full volume and then opened every window so that everyone heard it. Mum reckoned they were all smoking hash, although she called it 'wacky backy'. This music I heard coming from the car park was different, sort of hard and raw, like rock, but slightly softer and more melodious, and the singer's voice had an energy and anger to it. But it was something about the lyrics that hooked me:

London calling to the faraway towns,

Now that war is declared and battle come down

London calling to the underworld,

Come out of the cupboard, all you boys and girls.

When the song was over a DJ said that the singer's name was Joe Strummer and the band was called The Clash. A thrill ran through me and I whispered the words to myself again and again as the music went round in my head. When I sat down again at my desk, I looked at the equation and it meant nothing. Where before my brain was able to grasp the concept of X squared divided by 4Y, I saw only numbers and figures and I was struck by a revelation that what I was attempting to learn was meaningless nonsense. That was the beginning of the confusion. I didn't mention it to Mum, she would have killed me.

In the weeks leading up to the exams I was haunted by that song. As it got closer to exam time I found myself unable to concentrate on revision, and when I tried to absorb information it all became a confused jumble – dates, names, places, sizes, dimensions. I continued pretending to study, because I had no choice, not with Mum looking over my shoulder all the time. So I carried on even though I knew it was useless. Part of me was terrified of failing, but another part, a sort of distant voice inside my head, reminded me of *London Calling*, and this reassured me. Do you know what I'm saying?

UNCOMMON SENSE

Scent of ether is terrible
but familiar,
lingers on my mind,
eau de hospital
eau de childhood.

Oh the needles
by nurses wheedled,
pricks, blood and bruises
though too young
to be a 'user'.

Taste of nothing
starved I stared
at everyone having breakfast
free to feed
while I ate hunger and isolation.

I heard
the talk about me
as if I wasn't there
the ignorant questions
of those supposed to care.

Rows of rooms with windows for walls,

bodies distorted, contorted,

bloated and bald,

all mind's eye photographs

of my pincushion days.

Bayveen O'Connell

THE ROUGH SHORE

Kevin Boyle

Her cries are going through me like an indictment. It's the early hours of the morning and I wake to hear her in the next room. My mother is whispering to her, trying to calm her, but this urgent grief is beyond mere consolation. Dad said, "Take up your bed and walk". I know he's trying to cheer us all up but, this time humour doesn't help. I'm lying on a mattress on the floor. The house is full. The beds are full and I am the youngest.

I've never heard an adult cry before, not like this anyway. I've seen my mother shed a few tears but this is different. The woman is ripping herself apart. She's causing physical pain. A terrifying wail starts as a hoarse moan in her stomach and claws its way to a shrill, unearthly height somewhere above her. I am shivering. I don't want to see her like this. I pull the blanket over my head and sing something to myself, anything to block out those other sounds. I am seven years old and I've never heard of grief or its stages. I don't comprehend the saying "time can heal anything". Two days ago my aunt was normal; now she's lost her mind.

It was July in the late Sixties and a scorcher of a summer on our Atlantic coast. What a place to be a kid: to run free over sand and field, mountain and narrow, hot-tar roads. Our parents were a naive bunch who had never heard of stranger danger. Everywhere within walking distance was safe, accessible and free. Our daily movements were governed by the tides. We had the choice of three beaches, all suitable for swimming at different stages. When the tide was in, there was a lagoon and a surf beach. When it was out there was a deep channel cut out of the edge of the dry strand. We crossed the peninsula, masters of our own day. Sometimes we made it home for tea, but it was summer and often a meal was whatever you could lay your hands on. "Salad weather" – meaning thickly cut sliced ham, tomato and white bread.

"Run up to the shop, put it on the bill."

Come to think of it, I don't remember summers that were wet or miserable or cloudy, but they must have happened. Maybe vivid memories are encoded in our brains more powerfully in the presence of sunshine.

When I think of my uncle, the memory is always of myself looking up from below, about three feet below. He's standing on the kitchen table painting those corky aeroboard tiles we used to have on the ceiling. He's painting my name, and he has a splash of sky-blue paint on his nose. An extremely tall and handsome man, smiling a clean, white smile, always from somewhere above me. The physical distance between us is now frozen in time and memory. Had he lived, we would have closed that gap – me growing taller and facing him squarely as a man, him possibly shrinking a little with age. Time, fate, whatever, all conspired to make it the way it is. I'm looking up, always.

A child will take to certain adults instantaneously. Grown-ups try and define the attraction; children don't have to, they just know. There's a lot of wisdom in just knowing. My uncle had that way, and we kids knew. He entered our space, spoke our uninhibited language and, though he towered above me, he was always down there with me. I think he always has been. I had just forgotten him for a while.

My aunt had married late and was a good many years his senior. The exact number of years was a closely-guarded secret. It was clear that she was smitten and couldn't believe her good fortune to have found such a man.

"He's younger than me, you know," she would whisper proudly.

He was good to her and he made her laugh.

They were both really taken with their nephews and nieces, but they never had children of their own. So every summer they left their flat in central Glasgow, packed their bags and their car, and drove to Stranraer to catch the ferry for Ireland.

My aunt often mentioned my uncle's Lithuanian ancestry, something that added to his heroic status. Lithuania, one of the Baltic states – I had learned at school – was for centuries denied its independence by its giant, oppressive neighbour, Russia. Our wildly

Republican teacher had compared Lithuania's story to that of Ireland, and in my mind I imagined my uncle: the freedom fighter. I could see him out there battling against the vastly superior forces of the Tsar or Stalin, trudging gallantly through a snowstorm, carrying over his shoulder a fallen comrade, their bright red blood melting a trail in the snow.

In truth, I think his Baltic blood was about an eighth of his ancestry. The rest of him had its roots in the depressing sandstone city of Glasgow, where life was almost as precarious as in eastern Europe, but somehow not as romantic. There, you were very liable to get a broken bottle in the neck, for being either Protestant or Catholic. But that was old stuff to me and not in the least exotic.

I lived in a small, fast-decaying seaside resort with two shops and a caravan park, beside the beautiful expanse of sand and surf we called the Rough Shore.

There were massive sand dunes, an old church and a sailor's grave, a blue rock and a shelly valley. There were miles of sandbanks and bent grass with little, sheltered, mossy bunkers where courting couples hid, only to be followed and surprised by mischievous children.

Late July was the height of the season and, because of the good weather, the beach was thronged every day. Lots of families lived for a week or two squashed into small caravans, fighting for space, pillows, mattresses and calamine lotion. They came from all over, but mainly from the cities of Dublin and Belfast. Year after year they made their pilgrimage to the western seaboard, to the peace and the quiet – and proceeded to wake it up. They frequented the same two seaside pubs and sang the same songs and enjoyed themselves thoroughly. They were wise guys. They were cute hoors. They were city slickers. They wore the latest in fashionable clothes. Whatever 'came in' that winter, we had already seen on the visitors of that summer.

The evening before it happened, I remember our house in its usual state of summer madness. The day had been hot and the kitchen was full of sunburnt people. Somebody was washing dishes. Two sisters were negotiating plans for that night but were getting nowhere. My mother was somehow caught up in the crossfire, being questioned about a blouse. She was looking perplexed and answered honestly that she'd never laid eyes on the missing garment. A minor argument ensued between a dish-washing sister and a free-handed one. A cup fell to the ground and broke. Voices were raised further. My father stepped in from somewhere to restore order of sorts. The bedlam lost its confrontational edge. Now the atmosphere returned to that of a crowded school reunion, where people hadn't seen each other for years, and yet were in a hurry to catch the next bus. My mother always maintained that she could never get a word in edgeways when we were all together.

There was a television in the corner and somehow, through the conversations, accusations, pot rattling and cup smashing, I was actually following something. I think it was *Mission Impossible*, and if it wasn't, it should have been. My father reckoned I could lip-read. As the evening progressed the crowd thinned out. My mother climbed the stairs to her room to escape the mêlée. My father climbed the hill to the pub for his release. The rest of my siblings went rattling on and out the door, down the hill to the shore, where the other kids congregated.

My aunt and uncle doted on me and brought me everywhere with them. We went to strange places out in the country to meet relatives my parents had never even seen. These were people who lived inland in a rural desert I knew nothing about, in places where there was no view of the sea and that seemed strangely silent and lifeless.

We travelled in a tinny Austin 1100 with red plastic seats. The exterior was grey and inside it had a shiny wooden dashboard. For years the clock from that Austin lay in the spare room of our house. I don't know why my uncle had removed it. It was a strange and misplaced gem. It had been designed in a cylindrical shape to fit deeply into the dashboard with just the round face of the clock displayed. The brass winder protruded about three inches from the body. The face had luminous numbers. I used to watch it at night, when banished to the extra room by the presence of visitors. It was meant for something, a fine piece of engineering I'm sure, but it didn't fit anywhere. It lay awkwardly on its side and glowed in the dark – my own disabled beacon, marking the minutes of the present and future yet always guiding me back to the past.

"So son, where are we for tomorrow then?"

"I want to go swimming."

"Well swimming it is then," he said.

"I'd like to go to the calm shore, love. It'll be quieter there than on the main beach."

My heart sank at my aunt's words. The calm shore was flat and lifeless. You had to walk miles to get to the water and then it was only up to your ankles. There were no waves, for God's sake. I loved the relentless crashing of the waves. The way they knocked you about, pulling you in several directions, breaking on your head, sending you shooting to the bottom, from where you had to push yourself back through the froth, gasping for air, your heart pounding. Then screaming, laughing, whooping and diving right below them, avoiding most of their violence and coming up behind them in a momentarily tranquil strip of ocean, leaving you facing the broken surf, then turning back to face the next oncoming swell.

Besides, the lads would all be at the Rough Shore. No self-respecting boy from our village would be found dead on the calm shore on a sunny day. There were no shops near the calm shore, no pinball, no one-armed bandits, no chip shops and no cones. This was a disaster, I thought, and I don't care if it shows.

My uncle was quick to notice and said: "Oh-oh, I think someone wants to go to the main beach." He really couldn't have missed my forlorn look.

"Oh no, that's okay, I don't mind.... really."

At this stage my aunt interrupted: "Now son, it doesn't matter to me at all. Tell me honestly, where would you prefer to go tomorrow? Would you like to go to the main beach?"

"Yes, Auntie, I would."

With these words I sealed the awful fate of one of the giants of my childhood. The years have given me logic, reason and distance to disperse the guilt. But for years the child that made that decision blamed himself for the death of a loving uncle. Even today the facts remain. I chose, and he died.

I didn't stay with them very long that day. One ice-cream cone and I was gone. Oh, I splashed about a bit with him in the shallows, but when my pals arrived, I was gone. My aunt didn't swim but she was happy to sit on the beach reading. It seemed everyone we knew was there at some stage that day. My aunt and uncle chatted to local people. They were well known in the area through their annual visits. They had been out the night before to a singsong. People admired their singing. They used to do harmonies.

The commotion built slowly, but soon became blind panic. The adults weren't making much sense. There was a lot of running and shouting and some women were crying. Two girls had been brought in, they said, but now others were in trouble. Ashen-faced people stretched themselves to look out to sea, gripping loved ones. Questions. Everyone was asking questions and no one seemed to be answering.

The disaster was well under way by the time I reached my aunt, who was flanked by two local women. She was almost hysterical. She grabbed me.

"Have you seen your uncle? Have you seen him?"

"No," I said. "No...No...No."

Panic, and an unhinged sense of blame were already gathering in my head. I felt everything was out of control and about to burst.

The women took my aunt off, trying to calm her with reassuring words, but she pulled against them and sobbed. They moved her away.

I was left standing, looking after her. I was alone, confused, but certain something was very wrong.

"Drowned."

I heard the word "drowned".

It seemed to be on everyone's lips as they spoke in hushed or agitated voices and shuffled past and over me. I didn't understand the concept "to drown". I knew it had to do with water, going under water, losing control somehow, flailing around in the water, shouting for help – "Help me, I'm drowning!" The gap in my comprehension was this: I didn't know "drowned" equalled "dead".

When they brought him in, someone tried to revive him. A large crowd was gathered. At first I could see very little through the legs of the onlookers. Then I realised it was my uncle's head I saw on the sand. His bald head and a splash of blood.

They were crouching over him, doing something to him there on the beach, but I recognised him immediately. Numbed and light-headed, I ran screaming from the beach, seized by the most awful terror. I don't remember what or who I saw on the way to the house, whether I crossed the fields or went by road. The next memory I have is running into the house through the back door and straight into the kitchen.

"He's drowned. Uncle Frank is drowned."

One of the girls grabbed me and tried to calm me down, but I couldn't stop.

"He's drowned, he's drowned."

"What are you saying? Is he dead?"

"No," I screamed. "He's drowned."

Someone was dispatched to make sense of my story.

They discovered it was true. Frank had drowned. An excellent swimmer, he had gone to the aid of the beach-guards that day to help two girls who had got into difficulties. With his help the girls had been saved, but on his return he'd discovered that someone else was in danger. He had immediately headed out to save that person, but was soon overwhelmed.

They said later it could have been his heart.

The days following the drowning were long and dark. Then the weather broke and we had the first rain in weeks. I watched the dismal grey sheets of rain through fogged-up windows.

My aunt slept in the back room, in the bed she had shared with him. Her crying filled the house during the day and woke us from our sleep at night.

At the funeral I got detached from the rest of the family outside the church. I looked around and everyone was gone. A neighbour spotted me and gave me a lift to the graveyard. They were kind people, but they were laughing during the journey. How could they possibly be laughing at a time like this?

I stayed in the car – afraid.

Afraid of the coffin. Afraid of the grave.

I stayed in a stranger's car because I was afraid to see my aunt.

I couldn't watch her falling apart at the grave of the man I had killed.

THE SEA

Waves of blue

greeny blue and deeper blue

froth tipped,

lashing,

lashing eternally against the cliffs.

The beach wears

a mantle of contentment

always renewing,

forever young.

I climb up the cliffs

my eyes smart

from the salty air,

I hold on,

my fingers cling tenaciously

to hard rocks.

Down below

the waves are lashing,

lashing eternally,

I look down

into those turbulent waters,

blue and greeny blue,

I feel their turmoil,

I feel their depths.

Fingers numb from the clinging,

pain increasing,

hard rock boring into flesh.

I hear the swish and groan

of the waves,

pain increasing,

I can't hold on.

I let go,

down,

down into those greeny blue depths

of turmoil and chaos.

Then I see you

walking on the waters.

Mary Kane

THE CARPETEERS

Karen O'Shea

"Oh, Juventus, not over the rainbow again – I can't bear it!" said Laura in a high-pitched squeal. "The last time we did this I was sick for days."

Floto, short for Florentina, spoke up quietly from the back of the carpet: "Do you know, I much preferred the blue one – pink is such a girly colour." Florentina surprised everyone now and then with her 'out of the blue' comments. She was slightly obsessed with colours, particularly blue. She had on blue gloves, a blue scarf, blue hat and everything on the inside black. A strange girl to say the least.

"Look, we have to go where the carpet takes us," snapped Laura (otherwise known as Laura Bán, blond-haired Laura, to distinguish her from Laura Dubh, dark-haired Laura). "We need to hold on and see where it takes us this time, and Floto please, for once, just leave your obsession with colours at home."

Maria could see that it was going to be another long evening. The two Lauras were already squabbling and Floto was picking shreds of cat hair out of the carpet, counting to herself as she did so: "one for me, one for Blue, one for me, one for Blue". Blue in this case was her imaginary friend who travelled everywhere with her.

The carpet began its steep ascent, climbing slowly and magically through the evening sky. The higher it got, the smoother the journey became. All four girls lay back and began to settle into the carpet's rhythm. It certainly had that 'up, up and away feeling'. To go from relaxing on your bedroom floor to hovering at 3,000 metres was no mean feat for anyone, even the most experienced of *carpeteers*. However, these four were so accustomed to taking off and landing that, as soon as they managed to stop squabbling about where they might end up, who should sit at the back and who would be first off, they generally enjoyed the trips immensely.

Carpeteering was fast becoming quite a popular activity among the Guggles (those known as the searchers of space) and every family seemed to feel a little left out if they didn't have at least one *carpeteer* in the family. The Fuggles were lucky to have two, Laura and Florentina, and the Maggles had Laura and Maria. Maria Maggle was fast on her way to becoming one of the first Maggles to be able to travel beyond the 3,000-metre limit, because beyond that was *intraspace*, the space between inner and outer space. *Intraspace,* well, that was another world and Maria couldn't wait to get there.

Soon the carpet began to slow to a steady crawl, the pink now radiating against the clouds and bringing a kind of light dusty hue to the atmosphere. Floto was still busily counting quietly to herself, and the two Lauras were comparing just how sick they had been after the last trip. It was Maria who first spotted the other carpet – it was coming towards them at zoom pace and was surely carrying far too many passengers to be safe. It was time to act, but Maria froze. There she stood at the edge of the carpet, mouth hanging wide open and her hands covering her eyes. It suddenly went very dark.

Maria opened her eyes when she heard her sister Laura scream. Her shrill voice was enough to send shivers down anyone's spine, that is, if one was woman enough to have one. As an aside you might want to know that 'Searchers' are born with only a spine stem and that their spines grow through hard work and adventure. The spines of the four girls were of various lengths and strengths, with Maria's (she being the most experienced *carpeteer*) at least three centimetres longer than the others. The fact that she froze was later to become a serious threat to her getting her licence to go into *Intraspace*. She lost one centimetre of spine in that one action alone.

The carpet swerved dramatically to the left and then to the right before coming to a hovering stop, guided by the steady hand of none other than Floto who, having seen the trouble, sprang immediately into action. She stood at the helm, shouting orders to all three girls and to those on the other carpet.

"Don't anyone move abruptly," she screamed. "Just hold on to the edges, if you feel nervous. The moon will come out again in a few moments and we can see if there is any damage done."

The three marvelled at her composure, they couldn't believe that this was the 'ditty one', the one that everyone believed lived so deep inside her own head that she couldn't focus on anything other than colours and counting. But here she was commanding the situation with a degree of character that was admirable, in fact, it was beyond admirable, it was of 'spine-growing quality'.

Slowly, the clouds moved out of the line of the moon and the sky took up its lovely evening colour again. The four *carpeteers* sank into their carpet, delighted to be in one piece and able to see clearly again. The other carpet became visible; it was red, and its occupants were as varied as one would expect to find in inner space. There was a girl, a lion, a tin man, a scarecrow, a dog and a few witches hanging on the back. The girl, who seemed to be leading the crew, spoke in quiet voice: "Sorry about that, folks. We were just in a hurry to get home, and forgot that we're not the only ones flying over the rainbow these days!"

Dolly Mixtures

PURGE

Orange and yellow flames
Move gently toward her
Making her shiver and look with curiosity.
She stands, just about transparent,
as flames work furiously around her.

Her posture slackens
from licking orange and yellow flames.

Agreeing with flames of fire,
knowing how to humour and play
with each fiery red, crazy flame.
Fleeting thoughts run through her mind
knowing how she has forsaken words
and physical affection.

Orange and yellow flames engulf her.
Embers slowly appear.
Gone.
Still.
Unblemished.

Mary C.H.

A NATIVE AMERICAN IN LONDON
Phil Coffaro

Through the bulging eyes of this small-town boy from Adelaide, Wisconsin, London proved even more spectacular than anticipated. Buoyed by a sharp, adrenalin rush in those early days, I would frequently ride the Tube through this enchanting metropolis. I made several trips on 'the run' as I called it, covering Westminster Abbey, Big Ben, The Tower and Buckingham Palace. Eventually, I visited London Zoo, 'Madam T's' Wax Museum, even Dickens' House. Then, there were fantastic plays on in Leicester Square and Drury Lane. The restaurants; who said the Brits can't cook? The pubs? Absolutely brilliant!

I accomplished many of those exciting travels on my own, paying only minimal attention to my classmates who accompanied me from Wisconsin. However, as things settled down and classes commenced, I began to notice my fellow students more and more. One such character was Bradley 'Rise' Reizama. 'Rise' was a large man (6' 5", I believe) whose signature proved to be his tremendous, multicoloured beard. Rumour had it that, thanks to a short military career, he was over thirty years old. When queried about this, however, this 'mountain man' would only growl that it was none of their business. Except for these occasional unwelcome forays into his personal life, 'Rise' had a great wit to go with his gentle, fun personality. His greatest strength, to my mind, was that he had time for everyone, no matter the topic, its importance, or time of day or night.

Then there was poor Karen Watford. The daughter of wealthy parents, she proved to be nondescript, to the point of appearing downright uninteresting. Unaware of our lowly backgrounds, Karen – when given ample opportunity – would drone on and on about clothes, horses and even difficult servants. While we sometimes produced frowns of utter disbelief, she never did get the hint. Nevertheless, she was pretty, soft-spoken and genuinely pleasant.

And since opposites seem to attract, Karen turned out to be an excellent match for the gregarious 'Rise'. In fact, those two unlikely companions hit it off so well at the outset, they became 'an item' even before our group of fifty boarded the plane for London.

Easily the most intriguing member of our clique was Miranda Burns. At twenty, she was the youngest student on this trip. Miranda hailed from the Menominee Indian reservation. She always dressed extraordinarily well. Practically all of her wardrobe was hand made, courtesy of her mother and grandmother. Her striking, jet-black, shoulder-length hair complemented her immaculate, light-brown complexion. I sensed that her piercing, dark-brown eyes bore deep into my soul, adding a modicum of mystery to her already complicated make-up. To top it off, she would always wear the most beautiful turquoise jewellery, on special occasions.

I fell madly in love with this enthralling, young Native American woman. As a result, I contrived to hang around with her as much as possible. And since I got on famously with 'Rise' – nearly ten years my senior – it seemed only natural that we form a quartet: two guys, two gals. I did have to admit though, it was the most unlikely foursome ever!

However, as the naysayers correctly predicted, Karen and 'Rise' eventually drifted apart. 'Rise' bolted at Karen's clumsy attempts to include him in her insatiable desire to see first-run plays. Then, the King's Arms pub convinced 'Rise' to play on their rugby team, even though the big man had scarcely heard of the sport before our arrival. The idea of her man participating in such a "sweaty, muddy and violent activity" offended her pristine nature. Within weeks, our inseparable 'gang of four' had been halved to just Miranda and me. I didn't complain much.

To be honest, I always felt Miranda could have chosen richer friends. In addition to Karen, there were several other well-bred students from our lot. Chief among them were two preppy twin brothers, Timothy and Thomas Berger. Their father was some legendary politician, a regular household name in our neck of the Wisconsin woods. Then there was Jeanne La Blanche, the adopted daughter of the chief executive of a local insurance company. Now, they never appeared at a loss when it came time to fork out money for clothes, meals and entertainment.

The best Miranda and I could manage was to pool together our pitiful, prepaid weekly allowance. Still, we always seemed to produce the cash for that occasional cup of coffee, enticing snack, or even a pint of beer. As our term in London grew nearer to its climax, both of us found it necessary to spend a portion of our allowance on Christmas presents. After all, how could we depart this great city without a loud soccer scarf, a neat wool sweater or a snazzy cap? Miranda's dilemma was particularly acute, however, for, in addition to her supportive mother and grandmother, she felt obligated to purchase suitable gifts for each of her ten brothers and sisters. Thus, as the final weeks of our London adventure grew uncomfortably close, Miranda contributed little to our ever-shrinking entertainment fund. Yet, as a proud, determined young lady, she would have no charity.

"The last couple weeks, I'm gonna wine and dine ya, Paul, you'll see!" she swore repeatedly. I felt a little sorry for her, fearing that, for once, her pride had gotten the better of her and that she would be devastated if she couldn't deliver.

Before I knew it, though, that day of reckoning came. And, as promised, we dined in fine restaurants, attended some of Leicester Square's top-notch plays and drank in several London high-class pubs.

The night before our departure something gnawed at me repeatedly. Something about Miranda just didn't seem right, but I couldn't put my finger on it. When I finally discovered what had happened, my heart plunged into my unsuspecting stomach. Something was wrong!

"Miranda? What happened to your turquoise?"

Her quick, disconsolate glance at the floor confirmed my fears.

"Oh no, dear! Not your jewellery! Please, tell me you didn't…" I shook my head back and forth, before placing my face in my hands. An unbearable, sick feeling shot through my entire being. But, true to character, Miranda would have none of this melodramatic despair. Instead, she waved her hand calmly several times in a soothing fashion, then gazed deep into my eyes and, thus, into the furthest reaches of my soul.

"Hey, don't worry about it, Paul. 'Sides, what's done is done! C'mon, let's enjoy our last evening. OK?"

The remarkable young lady proceeded to raise her glass to the heavens, proposing one last toast.

"To us... and to the best experience of our lives!" she bellowed confidently.

"To us... yeah... that's it!" I mumbled in reply, voice cracking. I attempted to force a smile, but gathered that it appeared more like a grimace.

Within months of our return to Wisconsin, our once-wonderful relationship deteriorated rapidly. Essentially, what worked brilliantly in London didn't transfer back home. Exasperated by our falling-out, we simply returned to previous relationships. So, just like Karen and 'Rise', we ended up going our separate ways. It seemed strange, but the best we could muster was a friendly wave in the hallways of our school, or perhaps the occasional, amicable chat in the student union. Like so many relationships, ours ended up on the scrap-heap of unfulfilled dreams. Either way, wise or not, we accepted this fate in our stride, perhaps too easily, in hindsight.

I have returned often to London, where I meet with Fleet Street bankers, stay in five-star hotels and mix with the city's elite. Yet, I say nothing of my return jaunts to Ealing borough. Strangely, my feelings are mixed when I go there. On the one hand, there's the nostalgia and exhilaration of returning to the birthplace of my unsatiated desire for travel. Then again, I'm haunted by that inevitable anticipation of spotting the alluring, proud girl from the Menominee Indian reservation, resplendent in her lovely, hand-made garb. And, of course, her beautiful turquoise! Maybe some day, Miranda. Maybe some day.

HAPPY POEM

Did you ever try to write a happy poem
when you're wearing the darkness
and your breath is running a marathon?

Did you ever try to write a happy poem
when your fingers are in knots
and you've forgotten who you are?

Did you ever try to write a happy poem
when your skin is crying
and your tongue swells you into silence?

I did once
  On a cliff edge
    on a torn blank page
      in blood red ink
        it almost killed me.

Mitzie O'Reilly

Dolly Mixtures

RHIANNON'S GIFT

Rachel Webb

That spring Anna decided to use magic to find herself a garden. She was sniffing some perfumed green candles in the Euro Shop when Rhiannon said: "You've got loads of candles at home, why do you want green ones?"

Anna stroked the smooth wax, visualising her altar spread with an embroidered cloth, decorated with daffodils, smoke curling from the brass incense burner. She answered with the distracted air of a woman trying to hear distant music: "They're just for a ritual I'm doing."

"Oh God, Mum, all that witchy stuff, it's so embarrassing."

Anna looked up to meet the challenge in her daughter's eyes and flushed with irritation.

A month after Anna's ritual, some old travelling companions invited her and the children to move onto their land. The boys cleared up the field they had been living on, while Anna and Rhiannon packed down the bus, and they came to the place where Nick and Deirdre's low, white cottage stood guardian over twenty acres of mountain bog, above a forest of deep golden shadows, deciduous and lush in the summer dusk. Others had shared the land before, building a shed, which served as a bathroom, and running a permanent electricity cable from the house to a square of hard-stand in the next field, where Anna parked the bus. Before twilight on the day that they arrived, she ventured between shadowy trees down to the ancient river that polished the green to a radiant quicksilver as it lazed its way through the woodland's heart, forever uncurling between the roots and rocks of the shore. Surrounded by the scent of wild garlic, Anna lit a fire within a circle of salt, pouring a little red wine onto the earth as libation to the powers that provided such good fortune.

There was money to spare that summer – Anna had bought a

palomino mare, bred a good foal from her and sold the two for a useful profit – enough to buy an old Ford Fiesta and a separate space for her daughter. They had often stayed on sites where there was a spare caravan for Rhiannon to use, but this would be her own domain. A week before Rhiannon's fourteenth birthday, Anna drove into town and found her old friend, Billy, outside one of the chrome trailers in a grubby corner of the hospital car park. He offered her a fair deal on a sixteen-footer that was ancient and sturdy, a bit heavy to tow up mountains, but good for living in, and agreed to deliver it to her on the morning of Rhiannon's birthday.

Then Anna bought an extension lead that would take electricity to the caravan, a second-hand TV with integral video and a boxed set of the *Lord of the Rings* movies. The wall beside Rhiannon's bed was a shrine to male beauty featuring Johnny Depp and Colin Farrell, but mostly Orlando Bloom as Legolas the elf.

Rhiannon's birthday morning shone hot across the summer hillside. Not sure when Billy would turn up, Anna stalled for time by making a special breakfast of pancakes with maple syrup. The boys sat on Rhiannon's bed while she unwrapped Ty's box of chocolates and Cal's painting of the family, which focused on their tummy buttons and huge, three-fingered hands. When Billy pulled through the gate onto the patch of gravel, Anna watched Rhiannon's eyes open wide at the sight of the caravan. A workforce of Billy and his mate, Anna, Nick, Deirdre, Rhiannon and the boys manhandled it to the edge of the trees, out of sight of the bus, along a meandering track between brambles and gorse bushes that smelt of coconut in the summer heat.

That afternoon, when Rhiannon had arranged her few possessions in her new home, they packed a picnic and piled into the car along with the dogs. Barking, bouncing and singing, they drove between the narrow lanes of fuchsias, the two boys squinting at the widening horizon, shouting, "I can see the sea," long before it was visible.

When they had eaten their salad and most of the sticky chocolate cake, Anna sent the boys off with folded coal sacks to collect seaweed for her new garden. From her battered red flask she poured a cup of tea each for herself and Rhiannon, and they sat with their legs stretched out on the sand, silent for a while in the hiss of incoming waves, distant gulls crying out and the boys shrieking over a dead crab among the rocks.

Anna felt the heat penetrate deep into her muscles as she breathed in the faintly fishy sea air. Rhiannon's voice brought her back from reverie.

"Is it possible to make a person with magic?"

Anna dug in her bag for her tobacco tin to cover her astonishment at Rhiannon's sudden interest in anything magical.

"What do you mean exactly?" Anna asked. "Do you mean a completely new person, like Frankenstein or something?"

"Well, not a monster, just a being. Or maybe not make a being, but summon one from another world."

Anna finished rolling her cigarette and sucked in the smoke, picking a strand of tobacco from her tongue.

"It's not something I've ever really been interested in, but I read a book where this woman travelling in Tibet conjured a man. She wrote that he was a bit transparent but he was solid enough to act as her servant." She watched Rhiannon's profile as the girl gazed out to sea.

"But there are plenty of books about summoning demons and angels. I don't bother with that kind of thing now; I'm into something more natural, more feel-good. No desire for any more demons."

As Rhiannon smiled the sun shone even brighter across the glittering bay.

"No desire for demons at all, Mum." She stood up and stripped down to her bikini. "Let's go for a swim."

For the next few weeks Anna helped Rhiannon sew winter-thickness curtains, build cupboards from recycled wood and make the caravan cosy. With the autumn term, Ty and Cal enthused about their new class teachers, while Rhiannon moaned about school – the stupid rules and all the pointless homework. When she arrived home she would prepare herself instant chicken noodles, then retire to her caravan to wrestle with homework or, Anna speculated, to watch TV.

One evening towards the end of October, Anna felt more settled and began to plan her garden. After reading a story to the boys, she sat on the sofa, feet up in front of the burner, her lap laden with gardening books and seed catalogues. A rush of pleasure warmed her belly as she immersed herself in lists and drawings. Rhiannon came in, shedding shoes and coat at the door, waiting for Anna to look up from her work.

"Can I borrow a few of your books, Mum?"

"Of course. What are you after?" Anna thought that Rhiannon had long ago decided that all her books were boring or rubbish.

Rhiannon stared at the wood basket and fiddled with her hair.

"I wanted to have a look at some books about magic. How to begin. You know, how to do spells and stuff."

Anna felt a door swing open in her heart.

"Well, I'll give you a few that I think might be good for starters." She tried to be cool and not betray too much enthusiasm as she climbed up to her sleeping platform and shone a torch along her books. She chose three and handed them down.

"Thanks," Rhiannon said. "Can I borrow more when I've finished these?"

"You know you can, sweet girl."

"Don't call me that, Anna," Rhiannon muttered as she bent to pull on her boots.

Anna remembered Rhiannon once saying, "Everyone calls you Anna, but only me and Cal and Ty can call you Mum – so it's more special."

The following weekend, measuring the soggy earth with her short strides, Anna marked out where she would have the raised vegetable beds, the lazy beds for potatoes and the small, round herb plot near her door. After breakfast, Nick came across from the house to help her and the boys dig the ditches, laying the square sods over the oblongs that would become the raised beds, and then heaping the excavated soil on top of that. While the others sat on logs drinking hot chocolate, Anna wandered down to Rhiannon's caravan. Spacey music seeped out as she rapped on the window. The curtains were still closed, a crack of artificial light showing between them.

"What?" Rhiannon sounded annoyed.

"Hey daughter, I just came to see if you want to drink hot chocolate and help dig my garden."

After a pause Rhiannon said: "Sorry, but I'm really busy doing my homework. I'll give you a hand later."

So it was Anna and the boys who spread the new beds with alternate layers of seaweed and horse shit (all of which the boys had gleefully collected themselves), and stretched sheets of shiny, black plastic over the top, weighing the edges with the biggest stones they could carry.

"In spring that'll be lovely rich soil for us to plant our vegetables in," Anna told Ty as they scrubbed their hands clean in a bowl of warm water. "And next year we'll have compost from all our peelings as well."

"Gardens are 'sgusting," said Cal, winkling worms out of the ground with his fingers and sliding them under the plastic sheets because Anna had told him that worms were good for the soil.

She stood at the step of her bus and looked over the area where her garden was beginning its life, visualising a plastic propagation tunnel, trellises for peas and beans, rows of potato plants with their rambling yellow flowers, and the humming of insects. The future of the garden spiralled away through the years, like a speeded-up film of a flower's life, and Anna spiralled with it, ready now to stay in one place and focus on the details.

She found Christmas work in a local craft shop and Deirdre kept an eye on the boys until Anna arrived home in the early darkness. Rhiannon only showed up for dinner, disappearing back to her caravan immediately afterwards. Anna didn't comment, hoping to spend time with her during the holidays, but they rarely saw her even when school had broken up. Anna visited her repeatedly, inviting her to come and help make paper chains and cards, asking her what she would like for Christmas, telling her about a solstice gathering at the house. Rhiannon would never ask her in, but would open the top of her stable door and talk reluctantly, finishing the conversation as soon as she could. Anna felt the keen ache of rejection.

On Christmas morning Ty and Cal woke up at six. Once the burner was lit, Anna watched them opening their presents and made herself an Irish coffee as compensation for being up too early. Rhiannon came over at midday, bringing a present for each of them. Anna unwrapped a book entitled: *Living with your Teenager*. She laughed and said: "But I'm not really living with you, am I, Rhiannon? I hardly see you at all."

"I just thought it would help you to understand what life is like for me." Rhiannon looked hurt.

"Well, maybe it will." Anna intended to avoid any argument on Christmas Day. "Why don't you open your presents?"

Her daughter tore the wrapping paper off the biggest parcel and pulled out a denim jacket with removable fur lining that she had tried on a few weeks before, on one of her rare visits to town with Anna. "Oh, it's brilliant. Thanks, Mum."

Then she opened her other package to find a book called *A Compendium of Runes*, and a velvet pouch containing a set of runes that Anna had made herself, painting the symbols onto small circular pieces of wood that she had sawn from an ash branch and sanded smooth. Every moment of that effort was rewarded by the delight on Rhiannon's face as she reached over to give Anna a rare kiss and said: "These are totally perfect, Mum."

Now that everyone seemed settled, Anna started to peel the potatoes – they were going to eat with a bunch of friends down at the house and she was cooking all the vegetables for the feast.

The boys were engaged in some complicated drama involving robots, a pirate ship and a police helicopter. Anna said: "Why don't you make us a hot chocolate, Ree, and splash in some whiskey if you like?"

"Sorry, I can't – I'm going back to my caravan, I want to read in peace." She was already at the door of the bus, pulling on her wellies.

"But it's Christmas Day. You haven't spent time with us for months, aren't you going to have dinner at the house?" Anna could feel her throat tightening.

"If it's such a special day then we should all be able to do what we want," said Rhiannon, "and what I want is to read this. I'll get myself something to eat later."

As Rhiannon opened the door, Anna felt the constriction burst open in her throat as she yelled: "You're not even part of this family anymore, you never offer to help, you don't care about any of us. Just so long as there's food when you want it. I could drop dead for all you care."

The girl paused on the steps, speaking in an infuriatingly calm voice: "Don't get hysterical, Anna, I just need my space right now. I'm trying to find out who I am. If you read the book I gave you, you might understand."

With clenched teeth Anna said: "It would be a lot more helpful if you would just talk to me." She picked up the paperback *Living with Your Teenager* and flung it across the bus, regretting it before the book even hit the floor.

Rhiannon glared at her and said: "I can't believe you did that. And you wonder why I don't spend more time with you." She stamped down the steps, pulling the door closed behind her and disappeared between clumps of wintry gorse.

The weather turned bitter after Christmas. A dark and chilly cloud clung to Anna, shutting out the January sun. Each evening, Rhiannon came to the bus, ate her dinner in silence and left. After trying a hundred times to get her to talk, making jokes, sharing gossip, saying, "I miss you so much, Rhiannon, please let me back in your life," Anna left her alone. Occasionally, the girl would swap one of the magical books she had finished for another. Anna noticed that she had moved onto the heavier stuff now – Aleister Crowley, Austin Spare and various members of the Golden Dawn.

At seven-thirty every morning, before the children were awake,

Anna pulled the tray of ash from under the grate in the burner and emptied it onto the cinder path to Rhiannon's caravan. Then she returned to the icy bus and lit the new day's fire with a firelighter and kindling, waiting for the thin twigs to crackle before adding larger ones. Every time she lit the burner, Anna invited the light and heat of the fire to penetrate her loneliness. Without Rhiannon's company she felt empty.

With no savings left, Anna plodded through the bare forest, collecting firewood so that she wouldn't have to buy coal. She didn't notice how a wedge of sunbeams lit a clearing in the misty distance, two fallen tree trunks steaming into the golden air; she didn't hear a bunch of scolding rooks mobbing a falcon that had flown too close to their tree; she didn't catch the pungent wake-up smell of fungus as she bent to pick up a branch beneath a giant oak.

Anna took to sleeping through the grey days, waking in time to meet the school bus and prepare dinner. Once Ty and Cal were settled in bed at night, she often wrapped herself in her big coat and went crunching through the undergrowth of the silent forest. One night, she spread a plastic bag on a large rock, switched off her torch and sat by the river, watching the moon rippling on the water. Awakened from her dreaming by the snap of twigs, she caught sight of a figure moving between the trees. Intrigued and shivering, she slid a hand onto her dog's head and sat as still as she could, watching, hardly breathing, until the figure was only ten metres or so from her rock, then she pointed her torch and pressed the switch. Immobilised with shock, Rhiannon stood frozen and blinded by the light. Behind her, for a short moment, Anna saw another figure – insubstantial and white – like a shadow in negative, which seemed to dissolve into the air. Anna switched off the torch and, when she heard Rhiannon blunder off through the trees, away from the river towards home, she didn't call after her. Wrapped in the silence again, Anna was trying to decide what she had seen when a vivid memory flashed into her mind: Gareth sitting astride their black stallion, with baby Rhiannon laughing in the safety of his arms. Tears slid in cold streaks down Anna's face.

Next morning she dozed feverishly in bed while the boys prepared themselves a messy breakfast and Rhiannon grabbed a sandwich. During the afternoon Anna managed to get up, although she felt heavy and exhausted. Nick and Deirdre had gone to Dublin for a few days, leaving her in charge of their animals. While trying to milk the goat without its back foot kicking over the bowl, she glanced around the shed and noticed that Shadow wasn't there. When she thought about it she realised that she hadn't seen her dog since the boys had left for school. After scattering seed for the chickens and shaking Munchies into the cat's bowl she returned home, calling all the way, worried already because Shadow hadn't disappeared for more than ten minutes since she was a puppy.

Anna spent several hours trudging in ever-expanding circles, calling and calling until she was hoarse. She caught herself thinking: 'I don't know if I can bear to lose Shadow as well as Gareth and Rhiannon'. Gradually she slowed until she was standing in the freezing rain, only then allowing herself to realise: 'somehow I have lost Rhiannon, and everything is shit'. She staggered down a bank and landed on her knees at the foot of a beech tree. Holding a branch, she hauled herself up and began to pick her way downhill towards the river. In the woods the sky glowed green between the leafless trees and the air and the ground shone deep red, as if blood had rained down and soaked the leaf mould under her feet.

She squatted by the water, crying, soaked through and thought; 'I have to get a grip'. She searched for twigs and marked out a circle on the pebbly bank of the river, guessing where to place bigger stones for the four directions. Once the circle was complete, Anna walked around and around its perimeter, chanting herself into a trance. She called upon the guardians of the quarters, the deities and her own allies and helpers, asking them for freedom from her bleak view, to have her daughter's love again, and to find her dog. She stamped and shouted, crying and dancing a mad dervish step within the circle, then pleading on her knees, in a rush of words: "Oh Mama of Everything, oh Lord who is Beloved, King of my Heart, Prince of my Hunger, oh Breath of Life, oh Sweet Sorrow, oh Kali Who Will Come for Me When My Time is Done, oh Shining Light Beyond All Darkness, I charge you to help – lift me up and make it better."

As her voice and her movements got more and more intense, she wove herself into the tapestry of the river and the world above the river – the forest with all its life turning to stone in winter's fist – the warp and weft of the moment. As she drew the sky down to kiss the cold earth and reached out to every local thing that swam or breathed or flew, she bound the spell with a thread of words. Once the circle was open, she sank to the ground in an exhausted heap and sat there, watching the rain-speckled river sliding past.

Overnight the rain turned to snow. By early afternoon everything was white and she was out in it, calling Shadow, imagining her beautiful bitch injured somewhere, able to hear but unable to respond, freezing to death.

As she passed Rhiannon's caravan she heard a buzzing noise coming from inside. Puzzled, she opened the door carefully but the noise ceased the moment she leaned in to look, and she saw only Rhiannon's tidy clothes and her prize possessions arranged on the shelves. As Anna closed the door, she thought she caught a whiff of jasmine, or maybe honeysuckle.

When the boys came home from school they asked about Shadow, but they could barely stop long enough to change into snow gear before they were out again, screaming with happiness, chucking snowballs and building snowmen with snow cars and snow houses. As Rhiannon was leaving after dinner that evening, Anna said: "I'm so worried about Shadow, Ree."

Rhiannon straightened up, wearing one welly: "I've been trying to find her as well." She sounded defensive, as if Anna thought her responsible for Shadow's disappearance.

"I didn't mean that, I know you've been looking for her. I was just saying how I feel. I'm so lonely and I used to be able to talk to you about things. You used to be my friend."

"I can't really be your friend, I'm your daughter, and it's different."

Anna stood up and walked over to Rhiannon, reaching out and touching her upper arm. "But we could be friends, too. I believe that you do care about me. I just want you to show it. For us to talk sometimes."

Rhiannon bit her lip and bent down, hastily pulling on her other welly: "OK, I'll try. I'll try to spend more time with you. All right?"

Anna said: "I'd really like that," and let her daughter fly – like a bird leaving one tail feather on a cat's claw.

When they woke up the next day the snow was still falling and blowing into drifts against walls and fences. With no way of reaching the school bus, Anna settled the boys with paints and paper and wrapped herself in thick layers of clothing to go and look for Shadow again. She kept her eyes on the ground, checking for roots and hollows, wading rather than walking in some places. As she climbed up towards the open bogland, a familiar bark jerked her from a white trance. Two figures moved slowly towards her – a dog leaping through the snow like a dolphin through water, accompanied by the long-legged figure of a stranger. Anna cried out, "Shadow!" and ran forward, stumbling and laughing until Shadow jumped at her, knocking her over and whimpering with pleasure. When the stranger arrived he reached down to help her up and she saw that he was seventeen or eighteen years old, with pale skin and wisps of blond hair escaping from his Tibetan hat. He wore a green, hooded coat and green trousers tucked into high leather boots.

"Who are you?" she asked. "Where did you find Shadow? I've been calling her for days."

"I am a friend of Rhiannon's. I found your dog sick in the forest, I think she might have eaten some poison, but I fed her herbs and brought her back. She seems fine now, doesn't she?"

"Yes. Yes, she does. But… " Anna was trying to think while Shadow whined and butted her, licking her hand, dancing about in the snow. "Where have you kept her while she was ill? I didn't know Rhiannon had a friend here. I mean, living nearby."

"Well, I stay in a house in the forest sometimes. And I… visit Rhiannon."

His voice was lilting and soft, with an accent that Anna guessed might be eastern European, or Balkan, or maybe even Scandinavian.

"What's your name?"

"Bracken."

Anna laughed: "Rhiannon once told me that Bracken was her favourite name for a boy. Is that your real name?"

"No. She calls me that. My real name is hard for her to pronounce. And I like this name she gave me."

They began to make their way towards the bus, but Bracken stopped when they reached the caravan.

"I am going to visit Rhiannon," he said.

"Oh. Right. Well, thank you so much for saving Shadow, and bringing her back to me. Maybe you and Rhiannon could come and visit me later? I don't see much of her at the moment."

"No. She has been very busy."

As she walked slowly home, Anna glanced back over her shoulder at the caravan, but he had already vanished inside. Back in the bus she wondered how to deal with this new situation – a boy, probably a boyfriend, appearing from nowhere and 'visiting' her daughter. She decided to stay calm and not risk pushing Rhiannon even further away.

When Rhiannon turned up for dinner that evening, Bracken was with her. After they had eaten, he pulled a bottle of wine out of his bag and Anna found three clean glasses. He poured them each a drink then raised his glass: "To the return of your Shadow". Anna put some gypsy music on the stereo, which inspired Ty and Cal to do some crazy dancing while Bracken laughed and clapped in time.

Anna sat down next to Rhiannon and said: "I didn't know anything about Bracken until I met him with Shadow today."

"That's because I didn't want to share him. But he's going home tomorrow."

"Where is his home?" asked Anna.

"Oh, in a huge forest somewhere," Rhiannon waved her hand around vaguely, "in Romania, I think. He said I can visit him there next winter." Then Rhiannon leaned her head on Anna's shoulder, and the strange boy turned to smile at them both.

Later, as they were leaving, Rhiannon said: "I'm going to walk to the village with Bracken in the morning. To see him off. He's catching the ten o'clock bus."

"Are the buses running in this weather?" Anna asked.

"Yeah, on the news they said that all the main roads are clear now – it's only places like here that are still snowed in."

"OK. I'll get up early and see you off."

Before they left in the first light of dawn, Bracken handed Anna a small box.

"My mother sent it – a gift for you."

Then they were walking away, and she watched from the gate until they were out of sight, ignoring her fear that Rhiannon would get on the bus with the boy, remembering the feel of her daughter's hair against her cheek the evening before.

She whistled for Shadow and they began to climb up the bog track to high open land that had become a white moonscape. Anna swept the snow from a rock and sat down to open her gift. The box itself was carved from one piece of smooth wood with swirling patterns of dark grain that Anna thought might be walnut. Inside was a blue-glass perfume bottle with a silver lid. She unscrewed the lid and lifted the bottle to her nose. As she inhaled, she closed her eyes and saw a forest of vast ancient trees, people walking on wooden platforms suspended high above the forest floor. Intricate buildings seemed to flow and merge among the trees and a waterfall sparkled with rainbow droplets. All the people were tall, with a Nordic look to them. The air smelt of jasmine and honeysuckle, and Anna felt a warm breeze on her face, in spite of the chilly hillside where she sat. She lost herself in the pleasure of the scene and it took a while for her to realise how familiar it seemed – she had seen this place before. Lowering the bottle she searched her memory, staring into the space between snow and sky for a long time. Two ravens flew from the windblown trees on the highest ridge, croaking overhead, their slow wing-beats creaking in the freezing air.

The thread of Anna's thoughts unravelled. She laughed and sniffed the bottle again. As the sun drifted up the sky she became aware of how long she had been sitting on the rock and wondered what kind of mischief her boys might be up to, and whether Rhiannon was back from town. It had become a perfect day for potting early seeds. She replaced the bottle in the box, clicked the lid shut and slipped it into her pocket. With Shadow at her heel, she crunched back down the hill.

YOUR HANDS

Your hands
were work-worn,
rough,
ingrained
with minute
dark rivers –
deposit
of decades of
black spring soil,
damp summer earth
and autumn mould.

Your hands
lifted us
to see
small calves
in the corner
of the stable
where your
cherished horse
stood sentry,
contentedly
chewing
dry yellow hay.

Your hands
awoke
grey embers
below the
iron hook
where a blackened
kettle sang
before it spat
on strong dark
tea-leaves.

Your hands
scoured metal
milk urns,
purifying their
interiors
to receive the
evening's avalanche
of frothy milk.

Your hands
placed five large
Crunchie bars
above the
old worn wireless
to await our
arrival
on Saturdays.

Your hands
that grasped
like iron
in greeting
now clasp
cold beads
in final
frozen
farewell.

Maura Gilligan

THRESHOLD (from a novella)

Tom Mullery

I

Nathan is sitting back down from the Time Vision ©. Blue light always surrounds him after these journeys. It makes one think of those old Christian paintings, Immaculate Mother and Stainless Child with orbs of fluorescent light, making sure that people understand the Big Picture. No reports have come through factually that these saints and God glowed in reality, at least, not since the New Testament of the Bible. And that's a shaky source at best. Also – crucially – Nathan had his own sources, much more reliable than the mere written word.

Nathan can see the past, or some of it at least. The past floods across his vision as if he were there in the body. This particular afternoon he had travelled back to Kingston, Jamaica, some time during the summer of 1975. Nathan not only saw but felt emotionally what was happening. Gunshots were bouncing and echoing, voices were floating about unedited, a heavy smell of weed in the moist air. He couldn't make any sense of what was going on. He felt people were hallucinating and that he had better move out before someone cursed him or he got shot by a stray psychic bullet.

Let me clarify a few things. Nathan is a researcher for the pharmaceutical giant, Ipfen. With the money these corporations have they can buy anybody at any price…

Taking an evening break from business, Nathan visits the Red Night Café. It is here that he normally meets his contacts. The scene is Edward Hopper's *Nighthawks*. Everybody is in the bar for a reason. We can't see Nathan's face because he has his back turned. He is served crystal-blue, Bombay Sapphire distilled London Dry Gin. Across the bar sits a hook-nosed, red-haired woman with a hook-nosed, grey-hatted man. They are engaging the barman in idle conversation; he looks harassed. Nathan wishes that the couple would just leave; it is the bartender he needs to speak to. He has lost contact with Chloe and he needs to rope her back in.

The old Clone Warriors have taken frightened refuge in the forgotten Sub Division. The new Clone Warriors, vastly superior, have been retained to hunt and kill their predecessors. Before the killing is the humiliation. Killing somebody or something physically is easy; you just rely on the technology. Killing somebody emotionally – psychically – now that's something else. But the new Clone Warriors are built for the job. The Dream Killers © are coming...

Chloe is sub-commandant of the Dream Killer Corp. She's come a long way since the advertising days; she doesn't look any older though. She can feel the beautiful greyness of her eyes and how it affects those around her. Going into battle she would appear to have one flaw – her porcelain neck is just too slender; a flying shard of masonry could snap it. What did they call it back in the 'survival' days? Tall Poppy Syndrome (TPS). Stick your head up and it gets cut off.

She leads her seven marauders into the outskirts of the forgotten Sub Division. This one is not going to be easy. She starts to remember the perihelion passage; she remembers an age before this one, a middle age that she was alive to. She starts to dream, she dreams the heliopause again, she remembers she kills by dreaming...

II

She is looking at a painting from an oblique angle. It is Raphael's 1507 masterpiece *St Catherine of Alexandria*. In it, St Catherine is looking towards a yellow tear in the sky. She is just back from a long journey and a blue haze surrounds her, a far-reaching look in blue eyes. Dreaming, gods come to light, goddesses alight on shallow plains, the eternal will look skyward. Knowledge of fear and destruction and helplessness. Chloe is dreaming all of this.

From Beauty to Eternity: St Veronica and the True Image was a tattered old book, half-buried in an old bookstall under a grey bridge on London's South Bank. The hand that smoothed its covers, the man who wrote it, the lady who sold it, all these small movements of time and money were more than an infinitesimal exchange of ideas. The soul received. A soul looks towards the collapsed sky – South London in the grey haze – dreaming the forgotten Sub Division and the slow death there.

Messages never blinded her; they just sneaked up like a confidence man. She remembered an exhibition she saw as a child in Chicago and a painting called *Nighthawks*. Who was that man in the dark hat, who had his back turned? He had a message for somebody or was trying to find out something. Everything there had a purpose; the created and built world has a purpose. There were no angels in the painting, perhaps it's not finished yet. She finds a book on St Veronica while idling through an old bookstall, the woman who possessed the face of God.

Now she is at a play with Nathan, *The Star Shoots a Dart*.

"Close those eyes, Chloe."

Nathan, now her lover for a time, begins the creation of her mythic life. Sitting hand in hand, the darkened theatre masks light movements. Eyes are closed in perfect darkness. A time beam is moving interstellar, blue light flashing through an open Third Eye. A hectic race of light is swirling and infusing…

"Open those eyes, Chloe."

Nathan now her lover no longer. Job done, they are still hand in hand, still sitting. Time is moving slightly, Earth time. Chloe is immobile. Curtains open for second act. An old hag, very old, well over 150 years old, a witch, is leafing through books at an old stall in south London. She knows what she is looking for. Reads aloud to nobody lines from different books that she picks up. She is creating a new tone poem. The more she reads the younger she appears. More lights come up. The sun is rising over the tower blocks in the grey east. Younger and younger as the sun rises, still reading, with confidence now, aged 25. Shawl thrown off, Venus Riding the Waves. Clothes falling off, Chloe seeing her own destiny here acted out in front of her. *St Veronica and the True Image*, chapter three: 'The Worship of the Morning Star'. *She that Lightens the Horizon of Heaven* – the old Babylonian Psalm – comes back to her, now making sense. To light the horizon of Heaven.

She opens her eyes. Nathan has left and the scattered audience is moving too. She reads about an old Native American myth: 'The Wind also survived on the face of the earth, everything else was destroyed. A child was born to a woman (from the Wind), a Dream-Girl. The girl grew rapidly. A boy child was born to her. He told his people that he would go in the direction of the East, and he was to become the Morning Star'.

LOSS

Transported back in time
the old home, home of my childhood
late May, air heavy with scent of apple blossoms
revelling in their delicate beauty
the whites tinged with pink
the pinks tinged with white
Gleefully I gather handfuls of blossoms
carpeting the earth

Too young to know that such riot of colour
will never bear fruit
Too young to know that for them
their span of life is over
before it has really begun
Too young to know that great grief is always
tinged with real loss

Years later, returning to this same orchard
May month
same apple trees still bearing fruit
still losing blossoms
Riot of colour hasn't known change
I've changed, I've known loss like the apple trees
I too have known the pain
of losing something beautiful

Mary Kane

THE MASK

Maura O'Rourke

I was sitting at the bar, nursing a solitary whiskey, when she came in. I couldn't fail to notice her, as did every other male in the room. Heads swivelled, eyes appraised. She was well aware of the effect her entrance caused – took it as her due. Rather than turn my head I watched her progress in the large mirror behind the bar. A tall, slim, beautiful woman, she sashayed across the black and white tiled floor. I raised my eyebrows appreciatively. This one was a looker by any standard. Her flame-red dress clung to her body like a second skin. Her high strappy sandals clicked rhythmically against the tiles. In moments she was standing next to me. Black lustrous hair, cut in a stylish, glossy bob, framed a perfect face. Carmine-coloured lips glistened, parted slightly to reveal white, even teeth.

If she was aware of my scrutiny she didn't show it, just calmly asked the barman for a gin and tonic with lots of ice. I turned towards her and chanced a smile. After a moment she returned it with somewhat less enthusiasm. The eager barman handed her the drink, almost reverentially. She nodded her thanks and sat down on the barstool next to mine. Her long, elegant, painted nails beat a steady tattoo on the mahogany bar. She picked up a small, diamanté evening bag and pulled out a pack of cigarettes. As her slender fingers extracted one I fumbled in my pocket for a lighter.

"Allow me," I said with a flourish. As she held my fingers to steady the flame we locked glances. Fascinated, I watched as she inhaled slowly, deeply, and threw back her head and released the smoke. It was like watching a theatrical performance, seductive, provocative.

"Michael," I offered.

"Cassandra," she returned.

"Are you meeting someone?" I heard myself enquire. Inwardly I swore; how crass, how obvious.

She glanced at me coolly. I was intensely aware of her head-to-toe appraisal. What did she see: a dark-haired, brown-eyed man, reasonably attractive, approaching forty? My hair and teeth were still my own and, when I sucked in my stomach slightly, I could carry off the illusion of a man still in his prime. I was glad now that I had decided not to change out of the suit that I had donned for earlier meetings.

She smiled slowly and answered: "No, actually I'm on my own". She had just left a party – too noisy, too overcrowded. She had felt the need to escape for a quiet drink and so here she was.

My eyes flickered towards the fourth finger of her left hand. The evidence was there, two gold bands, one sporting a very large and very expensive solitaire diamond. She followed my gaze.

"Yes, I'm married," she said. "You?"

"No." I shook my head. "Not any more."

"Oh." She nodded sympathetically. "Children?"

Again I shook my head. Cassandra obviously picked up on my reluctance and smoothly, gracefully, changed the course of the conversation.

Noticing that her drink was almost empty, I signalled to the barman to bring two more. He couldn't bring it fast enough. Cassandra had a powerful effect on men. Close up she wasn't as young as she first appeared. Her make-up was flawless, expertly applied, but the eyes looked older, world-weary, with a hint of despair lurking in their depths. She was well preserved but, when I looked into her eyes, I had the disturbing sensation of looking into eyes behind a mask. Mentally I shook myself and applied myself to the delightful task of flirting with a beautiful woman.

A couple of drinks later I became more reckless.

"So tell me, Cassandra, what kind of husband leaves a gorgeous woman like you to your own devices?"

She ground her cigarette into a nearby ashtray and replied tersely: "The kind that is no longer interested. The kind that is embroiled in a torrid affair with a younger woman." She tossed back her drink defiantly and looked at me with a hard expression on her lovely face.

"He is a fool," I answered.

"Maybe, maybe not." She traced the rim of her glass over and over with her manicured finger. "And guess what?" she continued, "She's pregnant." Her eyes filled with tears. Impatiently she brushed them away. The brittle veneer was now beginning to crack. I genuinely didn't know what to say – she was obviously deeply hurt. Rather than come out with my usual flippant remarks, I placed my hand over hers and squeezed it gently.

"I'm sorry," was all I could finally muster.

She took a minute to compose herself and haltingly proceeded to tell me her story in her low-pitched, well-modulated voice.

"My husband has all the right credentials – wealthy, a well-respected lawyer, the right pedigree. I had it all: a big elaborate wedding; the beautiful town house; the idyllic house in the country for quiet weekend retreats; several holidays abroad every year."

She saw my expression. "Oh yes, I had it all," she exclaimed bitterly. "Except for one vital detail. I failed to provide my husband with a son and heir. Even a daughter might have sufficed, but no, I didn't even manage that."

By now the tears had begun to flow. The flawless complexion was cracked and streaked with rivulets of mascara. Wordlessly, I handed her a handkerchief to mop up the external damage.

"My husband spent most of his time working and was often abroad. I was lonely and bored, so I eventually succumbed to temptation. It was short and not so sweet."

She half smiled. When she fell pregnant the lover had melted away. Panic-stricken, knowing that there was no way that she could pass the baby off as her husband's, she reluctantly took the decision to have a 'termination'. Unfortunately, there were complications and she was left unable to conceive.

"I was terrified of losing everything and now I have." The marriage had limped along and they had drifted even further apart. She had suspected for quite a while that he had embarked on an affair. Recently, when confronted, he had admitted the affair. He had also informed her that the other woman was pregnant and that he wanted a divorce. He had insisted that, until divorce terms were sorted out, they would both fulfil their social engagements together. Earlier, at the party, Cassandra became very aware of the whispers and sidelong speculative glances. Unable to take any more, she had left and sought refuge in this bar.

"Do you believe in divine retribution?" she suddenly asked.

I shrugged, discomfited.

"I do – now." Abruptly, Cassandra stood up and, picking up her evening bag, said: "I must look dreadful." She retired to the ladies room.

I wasn't sure that she would come back. Her revelations had disturbed us both.

When she returned, the mask was firmly back in place. We both made an effort to lighten the conversation. I was no longer sure how this evening would end.

After another couple of drinks, I looked her straight in the eye and asked: "What next?"

She knew exactly what I meant – no more games.

"I would like to go to bed with you," she answered. We left the bar and without any further conversation made our way up to my room.

There was a desperate edge to our lovemaking. It was passionate and fierce. At that time we both craved a type of oblivion. Lost in passion, it was easy to forget the past. Entwined in each other's arms in the anonymity of a soulless hotel room, nothing else existed. Eventually, exhausted and spent, we fell asleep.

The next morning I awoke alone. There was no trace of Cassandra. It was as if last night had never happened. There was a dull, throbbing in my head and my mouth was dry. I felt a keen sense of loss, which surprised me. It was never going to be more than one night anyway. Too tired to move, I lay gazing at the ceiling. My mind began to whirl with unwelcome thoughts. Thoughts I had suppressed for a long time. Just as Cassandra was haunted by her demons, I also had mine.

Unbidden, the image of my eighteen-month-old son flashed before my eyes: blond, smiling, reaching out his chubby little hands as he tottered towards me; my wife in the background, laughing in delight as she watched his unsteady progress, eyes dancing, fair hair glinting in the sunlight. The image wavered, shifted, changed – angry words were hurled like stones, there was shouting. Emma's face was white and strained, her eyes hard and cold as she held Sam in her arms, like a shield, between us. His eyes were dark, frightened pools anxiously looking from one to the other. He had begun to cry, bewildered by the raised voices and palpable rage surrounding him. I saw him bury his tear-stained face in his mother's shoulder, plump arms entwined around her neck as they turned to leave.

I knew what was coming next. It was unstoppable. My stomach churned. Ice clawed my gut as I witnessed again the horrific picture of my infant son, pale as marble, unnaturally still, lying beside his mother in the clinical, cold mortuary room. My son, whose existence I had denied the night before, whose memory I had tried to obliterate. A car accident. Just one of those things – nobody's fault. Only I knew better. My selfish act of infidelity had claimed the lives of my family and destroyed my own.

Clutching the pillows I tried to drown out the roaring noise in my head – my son's crying, my own desperate keening. I curled myself into a ball. I cried for my son, for my wife, for Cassandra and, most of all, for myself, buried beneath the mask.

DAFFODIL TIME

It's daffodil time again
and the stretch in the evenings
makes me think of the evening
we brought you to the church.
You would have been proud of them,
three figures in black leading us
through the long sunset.

And I expect the March rains to gather
about us again.
They'll not be so bitter as the day
we brought you to Scarden.
There's no comparison
to the cold felt that day.

It's daffodil time again,
and I think of how
you would have laughed at us,
filling vase and glass and jug
with flowers,
how you would have laughed
if you'd seen 'Jack'
trudge through the field,
face hidden by yellow flowers.

And I think of times further back,
before we knew to count the seasons,
before we grew to know
that there is often black
as well as yellow.

It's daffodil time again,
and we have almost learned enough
to begin to sense the circle.

Siún McMorrow

THE LAKE IN THE BOG

Martin Gormally

It wasn't as expansive as the Bog of Allen but, in our part of the country, it was large – three thousand acres of virgin bog that had been eroded on all sides by successive generations who came there to harvest their winter supply of fuel. Those who operated on the north side of the bog rarely met their counterparts from the south; it wasn't easy to cross the blanket of sphagnum moss and dwarf heather that concealed rifts so deep that a man might fall into them and never be seen again. Communication around the bog was negotiated by way of the low area where the peat had already been cut away and more level ground prevailed.

In the cutover bog was a water hole. Its weed-grown surface and reed-covered edges made it difficult to discern where water and solid matter blended into one another. It was a danger to the unwary, a place to be avoided, but to those of us who were familiar with the lake it was the place to fish. Summer evenings found us armed with long, pliable ash saplings, lines of cord, baited hooks and boxes of worms. We dappled hopefully on the surface of the water in search of perch and bream. The fish we caught weren't showcase specimens, but the thrill of landing one was as palpable to us as that of an angler playing a seven-pound trout. Fitted to the line, at close proximity to the baited hook, was a cork into which a goose quill had been inserted. Standing as erect as the periscope of a U-boat, the quill wobbled noticeably whenever a fish started to bite; this was the signal to strike quickly in the hope of hooking a victim. When take was slow, we became 'squint-eyed' from watching the cork: a term we often used between us as we cast eyes on young women.

On the lake was a solitary craft – it scarcely merited the name of boat. It was the masterpiece of one of our companions who had grown up by the sea and who maintained he knew all there was to be learned about boat building. Over a wooden frame he stretched a covering of hessian material and ladled it with pitch to render it waterproof. The canoe-type structure was fitted with a seat and two rowlocks; it was designed to be manned and rowed by one person only. I helped to carry it to the lake edge – it wasn't very heavy. When launched it lacked buoyancy and, as an afterthought, its creator fixed inflated motor tubes along each gunwale.

"Now," he declared, "she's ready to go. Who wants to come aboard?"

There wasn't a rush to accept.

"OK," he said, "I'll do a trial run myself to prove that everything is in order."

We watched with trepidation as he rowed out to deep water and we prayed that he would return safely. After the initial voyage we all wanted to take a turn; Jeff stood on the bank, a smile of smug satisfaction on his face; his reputation as a builder of boats had been vindicated.

From the opposite side of the bog a group of boys and girls came, by coincidence, to savour the lake air. They taunted us about our choice of angling equipment and our scant knowledge of the art of fishing. By way of response we held our catches by the tails and waggled them in their direction saying: "Here is the proof – ask the fish?"

"Can I come into the boat?" a slender girl whispered demurely to me as her more athletic companions involved in horseplay with our lads on the bank.

"Are you not afraid of drowning?" I asked. "This boat is no Cunard liner, you know."

"Not at all," she cockily replied. "If it's safe for you then it must be safe for both of us."

"Very well, on your lovely head be it," I said. "I hope you won't mind taking a mud bath if the old tub goes belly up."

"You may call me Judy," she added.

"OK," I replied, "I'm Tom. You'd be well to know in case you have to call on me to rescue you."

"Can I try my hand at fishing?" she asked as I landed a silvery perch. Who could refuse such a modest request from a beautiful young woman?

Relieved of the tedium of watching the cork I looked her over as she diligently tried her hand at fishing. Her skirt swirled, displaying a pair of shapely legs. Her freckled face was crowned with a head of the most gorgeous auburn curls, her neck was snow white beneath her open-top blouse.

"Don't you want to know my second name?" she asked timidly.

"And where I come from?" she added almost immediately.

"Now, why should I want to know that?" I teased.

"Just a thought," she responded, "I felt that having studied my vital essentials you might want to learn more about me. Anyhow, I'm Judy Spelman. I live with my family in Greenwood. Do you know where that place is?"

"I should," I replied, "I went there every summer when I was a boy to stay with my uncle Frank and auntie Nora."

"I remember," she said. "Then you must be Tommy Killoran. You've grown big and tall since I last saw you."

"You haven't done too bad at growing yourself," I ventured.

After a long spell of trawling she caught a perch. That made her happy. I gave her two of mine to take home.

"Do you think we're likely to meet again?" she asked as we parted.

"Maybe!" I said. "Now that you've outgrown your pinafores, I expect you sometimes go to dances. I myself go to the Palais on Sunday nights; I'll be glad to take you on a foxtrot if ever we meet there."

"See you, sailor," she taunted as she rejoined her companions.

Through autumn mists and winter snows, we met, we danced, we kissed, we courted. By the time fishing commenced the following summer I had been baited, hooked, played and landed. This time I approached the lake from the southern side accompanied by my new girlfriend. It was my companions' turn to cast wishful, slanting glances at us while, squint-eyed, they watched the cork for a bite.

"Good fishing, lads," I called as, arm in arm, we passed them by.

BEDTIME

Like a woman's naked body,
elegant and vulnerable–
the curve of his arched foot
after taking off the sock.

Anne T. O'Connell

FRANCIS AND ME

Julia Marafie

Francis comes to my room each night. The soft veil of grey Connemara light dissolves and he sits at the bottom of my small, iron bed, the patchwork counterpane of pink, sprigged roses spread out beneath him.

He stays with me while the moon is bright. We talk and laugh about the many things we shared for so short a time, and we weave a future that should have been, could have been, would have been. Sometimes I take my rosary from its resting place under my pillow and we pray together for the people we love. The blue, glass beads shine in the moonlight and Francis says they match the sparkle in my eyes.

He caresses my shrivelled shoulders and threads his long, cold fingers through my silver hair; his touch gentle as a feather, he traces the criss-crossed lines on my ancient hands. Softly turning my wedding band, he is waiting, waiting still.

One bullet sent him there to that dark place where I cannot yet follow. I was young then, with two small children clutching at my skirts and another still unborn. Over and over I hear that single bullet blast. I hear the thud on the earth outside. I hear the silence – followed by a gathering panic – shuffles and commotion as his fellow freedom fighters drag his broken form out of the firing line.

A trembling knock at my cottage door tells me it's my turn, my world has ended and he has gone from this place.

His comrades lift him awkwardly onto the wooden table in the middle of the room. Tenderly, with clumsy calloused hands, they claw at his rough, serge shirt in a desperate need to mind him.

The fire crackles in the hearth, casting grotesque shapes on the whitewashed wall. No one dares speak, lest the anguish engulf them. A tiny drop of ruby blood spreads slowly, evenly, across his shirt, seeping away his life; its task measured, focused, unrelenting.

Nightly for 70 years now, we have shone together, soul on soul, until the dawn arrives and the morning star beckons him back to the shades among whom he belongs.

Christy thinks I'm very odd. "Ah, mother, you're dreaming mad dreams again," he sighs – for Christy is a being of the sunlight. He needs the blazing overhead light of the midday sun and bright yellow daffodils, or dancing fields of golden wheat and huge smiling sunflowers, to inhabit his tangible world.

But Francis – Francis and me – we draw down the moon. We exist in that still silence before dawn – that place where love enfolds our dreams, gently cradling them before offering them to the waiting daylight.

WORLD TRAVEL

The phone rings
as evening news finishes.
It's morning here, she tells me,
that familiar voice far away:

As far away, it seems to me,
as the day her feet rested
in the palm of my hand
while her head was supported
by the crook of my arm–

the day her travels began.

Dermot Lahiff

DOLLY MIXTURES CD 2

01. *Vaporetto*–**Mary Gallagher** (00:26:49)
02. *Her Father's Ghost**–**Mary Molloy** (05:27:74)
03. *Transience*–**Paddy Donoghue** (00:54:06)
04. *A Great Team*–**Paula Daly** (03:32:19)
05. *Sweet Six-tina*–**Órfhlaith Ní Chonaill** (02:16:69)
06. *The Confrontation**–**Eileen Sheridan** (06:04:11)
07. *My FatherLoved Pigeons*–**Michael Clement** (00:52:42)
08. *Do You Know What I'm Saying?**–**John Cullen** (04:57:69)
09. *Uncommon Sense*–**Bayveen O'Connell** (00:47:16)
10. *The Rough Shore**–**Kevin Boyle** (05:21:27)
11. *The Sea*–**Mary Kane** (01:16:02)
12. *The Carpeteers**–**Karen O'Shea** (05:08:54)
13. *Purge*–**Mary C.H.** (00:41:31)
14. *A Native American in London**–**Phil Coffaro** (05:51:50)
15. *Happy Poem*–**Mitzie O'Reilly** (00:27:37)
16. *Threshold**–**Tom Mullery** (03:18:39)
17. *Loss*–**Mary Kane** (01:11:22)
18. *The Mask**–**Maura O'Rourke** (07:45:66)
19. *Bedtime*–**Anne T. O'Connell** (00:11:51)
20. *The Lake in the Bog**–**Martin Gormally** (06:47:06)
21. *Francis & Me**–**Julia Marafie** (03:24:63)
22. *World Travel*–**Dermot Lahiff** (00:23:34)

*These pieces have been shortened to fit on the CD. The complete versions are contained in the accompanying book. Recorded in Dolly's Cottage by Andrew Wilson. Sound editing: Andrew Wilson, Órfhlaith Ní Chonaill and Shay Leon. Disk reproduction: Shay's Studio, Loughrea, Co. Galway.

© Copyright remains the property of the individual writers.